Road of Ash and Dust

Road of Ash and Dust

Awakening of a Soul in Africa

E.L. Cyrs

SYMPATHY PUBLISHING, LLC
LONG BEACH

ISBN 978-0-9982062-0-2

Sympathy Publishing, LLC
Long Beach, CA 90808
SympathyPublishing.com

Dedication

To our ancestors whose sacrifices,
pain, and suffering gave birth
to our potential.

May we never forget them.

Contents

Free Music

Thank you for purchasing **Road of Ash and Dust**. As an added benefit I would like to give all of my readers a **FREE DOWNLOAD** of songs referenced in the book. The soundtrack **Ancestral Strings Acoustic Kora** is a collection of traditional, instrumental West African harp music that I learned during my travels to the continent. Enjoy while reading! Visit the site below to begin your free download now:

http://RoadofAshandDust.com

Prologue

As far back as my memory can carry me I've always been required to wear a mask. As a child, I can recall being instructed by my grandmother on how to alter my speech patterns and personality to be acceptable at the newly integrated school I was to attend. It was the 60's, and the era of busing, more than a decade following Brown v. Board of Education. Busing was still a hot topic of discussion and a tinderbox issue for many, especially in the South. I began attending public school a little more than a year following the assassination of Martin Luther King Jr. The atmosphere of this nation was a tenuous mix of fear, hopelessness, anger and resentment. I was acutely aware of the things that made me different, especially when it came to the color of my skin.

I was tutored by the adults in my life on how to "act" when at school or in the company of white people. I was tested on the fitness of my emotional intelligence before being permitted to venture out of the safe confines of our small, segregated neighborhood. There was no escaping the reality that I would be navigating a world divided along lines of race and class.

Questions concerning identity were thrust upon me the moment I began to comprehend the influence that the past has on the present.

Stories were an integral part my childhood. The men and women in my life shared freely. It was common to hear adults converse, in hauntingly matter-of-fact tones, about lynchings, threats of violence and injustice.

In spite of the social and psychological trauma ever-present in the periphery, our families dug deep to unearth the joy in life and living. The church was an integral part of our community. Everything from sermons to supper was served there. We practically lived at our church. It was in the church that my concept of service was first formulated. In our neighborhood and church there was never any reason to wear my mask.

The me I was required to be when at school or in town, felt like an oppressively censored version of myself. When returning home, the casting off of that facade was analogous to a great exhalation after having held my breath longer than is humanly possible.

As an adult, I moved to Los Angeles and I carried my mask with me. During the day, I functioned as a corporate executive, Mr. Cyrs. Evenings and weekends I was someone completely different, immersed in the cultural community of Southern California. During the weekdays, I planned, facilitated, oversaw and coordinated in the corporate realm of my existence. Evenings and weekends I drummed for African Dance Classes, directed Rites-of-Passage Programs, and taught youth about their historical and cultural heritage.

While the corporate job put food on the table, it was the work within my community that fed me.

It was during a weekend with children of one of our Rites-of-Passage programs that a young boy approached me with a question. He opened his inquiry by addressing me as

"Baba," a word in many languages which translates to "Father," but also denotes respect for an elder. From that day forward, the children stopped referring to me as Mr. Cyrs and began calling me Baba. It was a name that took hold and refused to let go. Over the years, people in the community forgot Mr. Cyrs and only knew Baba. The mask I had been wearing for so long was beginning not to fit.

The comfort and familiarity of my mask-free days in church as a child began to shadow me. The messages I received to be of service were ever-present in my mind. The more time I spent with my community, the freer I felt. I knew I was at a crossroads, but my direction wasn't as clear as I needed it to be.

Witnessing the fire ignited in the eyes of a child I helped gain a greater sense of self-awareness, made it impossible to not want to help more.

I ripped to shreds the mask of my childhood conditioning and closed the door on my corporate employment. The burden of being anything other than, truly, what my soul longed for became more than I could bear.

Becoming Baba immersed me in a life's purpose that gave me the courage for the sojourn to Africa written about in this book. By the time I boarded the plane heading to Senegal, I was no longer Mr. Cyrs, I was Baba.

The search and struggle for identity is a unique, individual experience for many of us. Not all partake of the rigor of self-discovery. It can be painful, unsettling, and challenging.

My desire in offering you a piece of my story via Road

of Ash and Dust is to hopefully demonstrate, with an unmasked honesty, that self-knowledge is a key element in our growth psychologically, socially and spiritually.

CHAPTER 1

AIR AND WATER

stirring the water in a pond will bring up mud

I sat caged, distressed, in a seat designed more for torture than comfort on board my flight from New York to Senegal. The whirr of the plane's engines was deafening and we were buried so deep in darkness that it was anxiety inducing. Sporadic turbulence was tossing my stomach into a nauseous churning.

We were stewing in our sweat, imprisoned by the noxious heat. No matter which direction I moved, bent or angled myself, I could not escape the discomfort of stiffening joints. Maybe it was the reckless abandon with which my unconscious seatmate's sweaty, slumbering body continued molesting my personal space. We had already been in the air more than three hours and had yet another five until arrival.

I stared out through the window of the plane into blackness, my mind doing what my body was unable, wander. Was this a fool's journey? Would I be embraced or rejected in a place I had never been, the land of my ancestors?

I had dreamt of this journey as a child. My identity had been molded around the idea of Africa as "The Motherland," a sacred soil from which my ancestors had been forcefully taken. Here I was now, a nearsighted idealist, sprinting full speed ahead toward a land I dreamed possessed all of the answers to my questions of identity. This was my sojourn to affirm a sense of self-awareness that even centuries of slavery had not been able to defile.

As a child, stories of the past shared by my elders never failed to hold me captive. I experienced many sleepless nights, afraid to go to bed after after listening to ghastly tales of what occurred aboard slave ships, of torture and the butchering of bodies. The retellings of lynchings that snuffed out the lives of men in our family were elements of casual conversation. There was no need for Grimm's Fairy tales during my childhood, reality was much more terrifying.

Through adolescence I was often accused by my peers of being too concerned with the past. My inability to disconnect from history often caused me to isolate myself. For me, the past and present were not distant relations, but children of the same mother. I felt myself immersed in a historical continuum rife with depravity and disfunction not of my own making.

In Africa, would I discover why I felt such profound empathy for those who had suffered enslavement? Would I finally be able to see, and understand, myself in relation to the land that had given birth to my ancestors? My deepest desire for this journey was to connect with kindred spirits and bond through our shared cultural identity.

The sudden falling onto my shoulder by the comatose head of my seat-mate startled me. Irritated, I shoved his body back over into his space. His head dropped forward as his chin came to rest against his chest. The bouncing of his body with the plane's turbulence did nothing to disrupt his peace.

As my physical discomfort grew I tried to clear my mind, but the closer we got to Africa the more my confidence in the journey began to wane. What had been a dream was uncomfortably, and rapidly, becoming reality. Anxiety quickly set in as I became more and more aware of how far from home I was traveling. I became even more acutely aware of things I had forgotten to do or pack before boarding the plane.

Desperately, I was seeking ways to escape the chaotic mental meanderings: sleeping, reading, humming, nothing worked.

I twisted my torso and stretched, trying to avoid my seat companion's sweaty body. I was not as fortunate as him. The ease at which he seemed to navigate this space and time had me envious. My mind was jumping, maybe because my body could not.

I stared out into the darkness more than 30,000 feet above the earth's surface. An awareness materialized. Directly below us was the Atlantic Ocean, undulating, breathing, alive. I was crossing the very same ocean of my enslaved ancestors, but moving in the opposite direction. There was something triumphant in this return voyage, more than 200 years in the making. It could be considered a coup of the human spirit that my ancestors survived the holocaustic three-month passage to America, chained in the diseased belly of slave ships. Even more than that, in spite of the evil, oppression and savagery heaped upon it, and irrespective of time, the human spirit was navigating its return.

I immediately recalled one of the most horrific tales I've ever heard. It was told to me by my grandmother. She recounted the story of an African woman watching the crew of a slave ship tossing bodies, the sick and dead, over the sides. Sharks that had learned to trail these vessels specifically for this reason, tore into and devoured the discarded beings. My grandmother's pitch would rise excitedly whenever she reached the point in the tale when the woman managed to break free, run, and leap over the side of the ship into a bloody froth of sea, mangled bodies, and ravenous sharks.

Over my lifetime I have thought long and hard about this woman, and the many others like her, who consciously chose an unimaginable death in the face of slavery. As I sat transfixed on the night's blackness, I imagined the floor of the ocean littered with the remains of these souls. I could smell the churning currents of salt water stirring up their settled remains, pushing them through the murky, dark depths.

The sense of triumph I had felt moments earlier began to give way to sadness.

They are still down there, I thought to myself. The bodies of my ancestors are still down there, buried beneath the mountain ranges and valleys of the ocean.

I sat motionless, staring out of the window into nothingness. A sudden streaming collage of faces, shackled hands and ankles ascended the black, watery canyons below. It was impossible to deflect. I closed my eyes, but their faces assumed greater detail, heart-wrenching expressions. I tried to distract myself by staring out into the dark sky, but they reappeared, wraith-like cutting through the night, reaching out to me. I was present, but not completely. I physically shook myself to pull my body back into itself. I forced my eyes away from the window and scanned the cabin. Every single person on this plane was black. It was surreal. Each person aboard the flight resembled the faces of those I had been closing my eyes trying to avoid. Never in my life had I experienced such hallucinations.

The plane hit another wave of turbulence, tossing us around in our seats. Normally, that would have been enough to shift anyone's focus, but there was nothing that could deaden the chorus of droning voices coming up at me from below. The bodies continued rising from the deep. My heart ached with a profound connection to each of the opaque figures moving up through the night. The sadness that had held me earlier was nothing compared to the pain brought on by this peculiar intimacy with the dead.

I labored to breathe as a small stone formed in my throat. Pushing my head back against the headrest, a current of despair slowly coursed through me. It pushed its way up through the thick obstruction in my throat, bypassing my clenched jaws and then out and around my head. I sat immersed in hopelessness. Again, I searched around the plane in an attempt to bring myself back to normalcy. Everyone was asleep. Everyone! The thoughts, the images became too much. The sorrow, overwhelming.

The dammed up tears broke through. Inhibitions decimated, I no longer cared if anyone saw or heard my mourning. I sobbed uncontrollably, my body convulsing. My heart felt like it was gripped in a vice. For more than thirty minutes, I cried myself into a state of spiritual and physical exhaustion.

As the emotional tsunami slowly subsided, my jaw began to unclench. My tightened fists gradually unfurled, removing fingernails dug deep into the meat of my palm. The images and voices vanished. Again, all that was before me was darkness and the tepid odor of foul, recirculating air. All that remained was an intense sense of loss.

There was a slight ringing in my ears. The interior of the plane faded to pitch-black as I drifted off into an overwhelming, exhaustive sleep.

Turbulence jolted me awake. Overhead lights were blinking on and off throughout the darkness. People were busying themselves in their seats. Without warning, blinding light flooded the cabin. The captain's voice boomed over the intercom. We were a half hour from landing and everyone needed to prepare. Half an hour! Had I been sleeping that long? My mind felt much more at ease but my body was beaten, bruised, sore and aching all over.

The lines for the bathrooms extended the length of both aisles. There were so many people! I found it hard to believe that every single one of them had been asleep during my episode. I self-consciously looked around and into the eyes of my fellow passengers to see if any of them registered a knowing glance of having witnessed my fit of crying. The indifference I encountered made it clear that no one was paying me any mind.

Glancing out of the window, it was still nighttime, but the light of the moon reflected brightly off of the ocean's surface.

After being trapped on this plane for more than seven and a half hours, the thought of setting foot in Africa was exhilarating. A lone soul was returning home, after hundreds of years in exile. The rush of adrenaline and the euphoric sense of purpose were all I needed to lift me up and have me looking ahead, not back.

The plane began its descent. Whether I believed myself ready for this experience or not was no longer relevant. There was no turning back. I was about to embrace a life-long yearning. I was only moments away from feeling the sacred soil of Mother Africa beneath my feet. Spiritually, I felt sure that I was realizing a dream for many who had been taken away hundreds of years ago, their dream of returning home.

CHAPTER 2

LES FRÈRES

follow a river and find a sea

The plane finally landed at Senegal's Léopold Sédor Senghor International Airport. Although exhausted and disheveled, I couldn't contain my excitement.

The queue exiting the plane lumbered along, coming to complete stops every few seconds. The air had been turned off as soon as we touched down. In spite of being trapped in an area rapidly deteriorating into squalor, my enthusiasm for having arrived in Africa couldn't be dampened.

I exited the polluted cabin out into a listless, stagnant heat and began sweating profusely. I was standing on the platform of a rickety staircase. The airport appeared to be a few hundred yards away.

The line down the steep stairs dragged on as passengers ahead of me moved cautiously to keep from falling. It was a painful joy being able to see the terrain from atop the staircase but unable to move towards it any quicker. Each step down set my heart racing just a bit more. By the time I made it to the last few steps, I was so excited that I almost slipped and tumbled into the woman in front of me.

As I took my first step from the stairs onto Africa's soil,

I purposefully led with my left foot. I had choreographed this moment many times in my mind over the years.

By touching the land of my ancestors with my left foot first, I was, symbolically, leading with my heart. When I brought my other foot down off of the final step, I was grinning ear-to-ear, celebrating that I was standing, feet firmly planted on African soil. There had to have been a glowing orb of light emitting from my body, or something, as a dangerous dose of joy and excitement raced through my veins. Someone related to me had been forcefully taken from this land more than 200 years ago in unimaginable pain, and here I was, their progeny, attempting to vindicate their soul. To say I was feeling proud would be an understatement. I must have looked like a statue of a peacock as I stood there with my chest poked out and head held high.

The yelling and cursing from the passengers behind me yanked my senses back into reality. I had stepped off at the bottom of the stairway and was holding up the line of hundreds of people behind me as I experienced my moment. I darted across the tarmac over to the awaiting bus and boarded. I hadn't been in Senegal 5 minutes and had already found a way to be disruptive. I kept my head down in an attempt to avoid eye contact with the people whose movement I had disrupted just moments before.

The buses carried us across the loosely graveled tarmac to a door at the back entrance of the main terminal. There were, quite literally, hundreds of us and we were being ushered through a single door! Once again, a painfully slow line formed at the door as Senegalese Soldiers began barking and waving their arms at us to move through more quickly. The sign over the door looked as though it had been hastily written and was held up by a strip of gray duct tape. It read, "Douaniére (Customs)."

There were a few among us being directed away from the collective throng and over to a set of automated sliding glass doors just a few feet away. The heat was oppressive and yet, even though I was a great distance from those sliding glass doors, I could feel the cool, air-conditioned breeze when it opened. As each of them entered the air conditioned room they shook the hand of the guard (the old "money handshake"). Although sloppily performed, it was still universally effective at changing one's situation.

I was now in the care of customs and would learn my first lesson in West African diplomacy; if you have money you don't wait in line. If you don't have money, lines are, specifically, constructed for you. I stood in line for hours before finally making it through customs and out of the airport.

I possessed a single name on a crumpled sheet of paper buried deep in my pocket, Sankoun. Badialy, a good friend from Los Angeles who was from Senegal, had told me to be on the lookout for his brother Sankoun once I exited the airport. He would be carrying a kora, a West African Harp, with the symbol of a bird decorating the back of the instrument's gourd.

When I finally exited customs, I walked out into a palatial room of high ceilings with a wall of glass exposing the airport's main entrance. There were hundreds of people waiting on the other side of a roped off area just outside of customs. I immediately spotted Sankoun carrying the kora. It was a beautiful instrument, elaborately decorated. He and four other young men stood just outside of the restricted area.

Sankoun stood about five-foot-six or five-foot-eight with long flowing dreadlocks. He was slender but muscular with an air of confidence beyond his years. His smile was wide as he led his group of four towards me. We all hugged excitedly, strangers to one another but experiencing a collective sense of relief at having successfully made contact.

Sankoun had arranged for a taxi, and it was waiting for us outside of the airport... down the road.

Down the road? I thought to myself, "Why down the road? Why not right here in front of the airport's entrance?" My impulsive, demanding, concerns for comfort took me by surprise.

I managed to shrug off the minor inconvenience of having to walk a bit after having been trapped inside of a metal tube for more than seven hours. Sankoun and his friends would not permit me to carry any of my luggage down the dirt road to the awaiting taxi. The sight of us must have been comedic. Here I stood at six foot two and weighing a very healthy two hundred pounds, carrying nothing. To each side of me were four slender, slight of stature young men loaded down with a couple of oversized, heavy suitcases. Every attempt I would make to alleviate their agony would be met with a brutal rebuff, "No... we are here to take care of you!"

I knew it was my responsibility to pay for the taxi. I had been tutored well by Badialy. I knew that it was customary to negotiate everything. I asked Sankoun what the taxi driver wanted to charge us. When he told me, I realized that

I would soon be out of money if I didn't jump straight into the cultural norm of negotiating. When we got to the taxi, the driver was sitting there in the dark, waiting, listening to the car's radio. I immediately approached him and introduced myself. He understood my broken French well enough to offer me a gaping smile.

Once the driver and I completed our pleasantries, I gently nudged my way into negotiating a lower price for the fare from the airport to Thiaroye.

My negotiating skills were very entertaining to everyone present. They were laughing so hard that we had to pause a few times just to be able to hear one another. Maybe it was out of sheer pity, but the driver relented to a lower fare, tapped me on the back and opened the car door. All five of us piled into a compact meant to seat only two people comfortably.

The little vehicle bumped, shivered and coughed as we made our way through the soaring humidity. If I closed my eyes and just felt the moist air and heat whenever the car came to a stop, I could have easily been in Louisiana, Mississippi or Alabama. If we had closed the windows of the taxi, which were inoperable, we might have succumbed to the constant flow of carbon monoxide. Beneath the rear passenger's seat was a large rusted hole in the floor.

We traded luggage, arms, and legs for comfort several times during the ride. The red clay dirt of the roads leading from the airport looked exactly like the soil of my childhood visits to family in Alabama and Mississippi. Dim lights from hanging kerosene lamps in doorways and occasional barrel fires lit our path. It was late in the evening but there were crowds of people gathered on every corner we passed. Our route took us past one dilapidated structure after another.

The taxi was kicking up red dust. I tried to imagine what it must have been like to come from this place and end up on a plantation somewhere in Mississippi. I heard stories, as a child, of slaves arriving from Africa and coming into contact with this familiar red soil. They would get excited upon seeing it and begin shoving handfuls into their mouths. Their attachment to their homeland was soul-stirring.

Occasionally we slowed, the driver navigating narrow passageways of shanties and concrete structures. Many of the roads didn't appear meant for vehicles. Fearless, silhouetted pedestrians thought nothing of cutting us off. The orange burning glow of cigarettes appeared like ubiquitous fireflies.

The smell of the air was thick with outdoor cooking, propane and burning coal.

An abrupt stop let me know we had arrived at our final destination.

Exiting the taxi was analogous to a classic clown routine. We tumbled, rolled and fell from the door. I was drenched in sweat, covered with dirt. There had not been any way of avoiding it. I swooned over the idea of a shower. Sankoun's friends began pulling my luggage from atop one another as they disentangled themselves from interlocking legs and arms to exit the taxi after me. It seemed as if I had stepped back in time almost one hundred years as a mule pulling a cart slowly ambled past us.

I stood outside and looked up at the rust-colored entry gates of the compound. These metal gates stood about seven feet high, and each door was the width of about three and a half feet. There was the head of a small lamp, similar to what a mechanic might hold in one hand while working beneath a car, dangling from the edge of a corrugated roof. Just beneath the light, painted atop the concrete square holding the gate in place were the words, "Les Frères (The Brothers)."

Apparently, "Les Frères" were a Sufi brotherhood who had owned the property before Badialy's father, Bouba, purchased it.

We had arrived. We were at the Cissoko family compound, and it was late at night. Sankoun let me know that I would be sharing a room, and bed, with him. My Western sensibilities were making themselves acutely aware as I, unconsciously and reflexively, began nodding my head "no." I caught myself mid-nod and stopped. I breathed in deeply and planted the thoughts in my head that I was here to experience another culture, not to impose my will upon it.

I exhaled as we opened the gates to a long, narrow, enclosed walkway. To my left were a row of four single room bungalows made of the same cinder blocks that formed the outside walls. Immediately to my right was a huge open entrance leading to a large, open-air area with a cement foundation. I would find out later that this was where the family rehearsed their drumming and dancing. Inside of this common area was another entrance housing a rectangular enclosure that served as the bathroom and shower. An old, cracked porcelain toilet sat atop a hole in the ground. Someone had taken the time to put a large empty coffee can in the hole under the receptacle. The shower? Only a few feet away.

The boys escorted me to my room. The surroundings were harsh. Cement walls, cement floor and a large piece of industrial foam sitting atop wooden slats formed the bed.

Again, I breathed in deeply and focused on my purpose for this journey. I was here to learn and, it seemed, there would be many opportunities presented to me. Fortunately, I had reached a point of exhaustion where the flimsy piece of yellowed, square foam began to look inviting. I hadn't rested my head but a few minutes before sleep overtook me.

Through the fog of my coming awake, I heard whispers and giggling. My eyes fought against my mind's impulse to open and look around. My head refused to lift or turn. I was in a struggle with myself somewhere between sleep and consciousness. Through the blur and haze of my half-opened eyes, I made out three figures standing in the doorway. The silhouettes of a man with two smaller figures, all holding hands, were standing at the entrance of my room.

I managed to sit up, and the two mini-silhouettes giggled loudly and fled. The young man standing in the doorway was Sajo, Badialy's youngest brother.

"Good morning Baba," he called to me, "Welcome to Africa!"

I was in Africa! Adrenaline shot me awake. I couldn't contain my excitement. I jumped out of bed. I felt a little light headed, but that faded quickly. My heart was racing. Through the window at the front of my room, the sun's rays cast a beautiful stairway of light onto the floor.

I had to get out of the room, see everything in the light of the day for the first time. I needed to breathe Africa's morning air. Exiting the room became part ritual, part celebration. The thought of seeing and feeling the heat of the sun for the first time on Africa's soil intoxicated me.

The evening's darkness had hidden from me a level of destitution that I was in no way prepared to experience. There were young men scattered all about the ground, sleeping just outside of my room. I had to step over them to walk through the tiny corridor of the compound past three other small rooms similar to mine. For some reason, I had an overarching desire to open the front gates of the small compound and see the view outside of Les Frères.

I opened the tall metal gates and stepped out onto a roadway. There were rows and rows of similar compounds, gated side by side and across from one another, sharing cinder block walls. The uneven, bumpy dirt road acted as a divider between the two opposing rows of these structures. Up the street, toward the main road was a minaret poking up over the walls and adjacent buildings. From the speakers on top, a loud, crackling call to prayer began.

I felt as if I had stepped back in time. I stood paralyzed by the magnitude of poverty surrounding me. The recorded Islamic call to prayer played as background music to a very unsettling scene. A breeze blew by me carrying the unmistakable smell of pungent urine. When I turned around to go back into the compound, I realized the conditions inside were even more depressing. There were stacks and rows of cinder blocks. I covered my nose and mouth with both hands each time the wind wafted the scent of sewage through the area.

It was in that instant that I realized something about myself.

My mind was racing, calculating the budget for a hotel, air conditioning, a swimming pool, cleanliness. I was simultaneously judging my hosts and preparing for a fast exit from my surroundings. There was something ugly in my thoughts. I could taste the bitterness. I was, albeit incrementally, becoming aware of an aspect of myself that I had never had to face. I thought I knew poverty as a child. I recalled standing in line, embarrassed by my brightly colored Free Lunch Card, but this was something beyond low economic standing.

Shame crept over me as I thought about whether I could survive two months under these conditions. The shame I was experiencing had more to do with the hospitality that this family had extended and my ungratefulness. The most dominant thought occupying my mind was that the people of this area lived here, and who was I to think myself above them? The money I had brought with me was supposed to be used for paying for my room and board and the lessons of music I would receive.

The thought that I would take this money that they may have needed and abscond to some hotel in the city sickened me. I attempted to repress this ugliness within me as I turned to walk back into the compound. I made up my mind. I would stay and live as my host family did regardless of the conditions.

As I was walking back to the compound, I was greeted by Badialy's mother, Momina and his father, Bouba. I wasn't sure how long they had been standing behind me at the gate's entrance. Bouba extended his hand, but said nothing while looking directly into my eyes. It was one of the most uncomfortable introductions I've ever made. I spoke,

"Je suis Baba et je suis tres heureux de faire votre connaisance."

I had practiced that bit of French, introducing myself, over and over again, at least a few thousand times so that it flowed smoothly off of my tongue. Bouba didn't seem impressed, his affect was flat as he stood motionless staring into my eyes and holding my hand tightly for an awkwardly long time after the customary handshake had ended. I trembled nervously. I felt as though Bouba was reading every single ugly thought I was having.

Momina interceded, "This is my husband, Bouba. I am Momina. We speak English."

Momina and I exchanged pleasantries as Bouba released his grip on my hand and stood before me arms folded. She explained that it was not safe for me to be standing out on the road so early in the morning by myself. The two of them ushered me back into the compound, Momina walking slightly ahead and Bouba to my rear, out of peripheral view. They escorted me down the narrow, open-air passageway to an area where three white plastic lawn chairs were waiting. Momina motioned for me to take a seat. She and Bouba stood in front of their seats. I was beginning to feel that the situation was becoming increasingly formal. I was not comfortable being the first to sit down and so I followed my intuition.

"Please," I implored, "I would not feel right sitting down before my elders have taken their seats."

Momina smiled but turned her head to the side, almost as if she didn't want anyone to see her reaction to my words. Bouba's face was expressionless except for the stoic stare burning a hole through my face. They sat first and then I followed.

Momina began peppering me with questions about her son, Badialy, back in the United States. She inquired about his health. She wanted to know what, and how often, he was eating. What the conditions were like where he lived? Did he have many friends? Momina wasn't leaving any stone unturned investigating her son's well-being.

I was making every attempt I could to stay focused, but I began feeling as if my body was slowly slipping out of itself. There was a strong downward pull, trying to divide my body from my spirit. I was watching Momina's lips move, but her words were fading, beginning to sound muffled.

"Go back to bed!" Bouba shouted, "Go back to sleep!"

These were the first words that I heard out of Bouba's mouth and they startled me back to full consciousness. Momina's questioning abruptly ended with her husband's interruption. When I gained my bearings, I found myself slumped down in the white plastic lawn chair, arms dangling over the side with part of my spine resting against the seat and my knees extended unflatteringly towards the couple.

Had I answered any of Momina's questions about her son? I couldn't say.

Bouba snapped at me once again, "Sleep! You need sleep!"

This time, as harsh as his tone was, it contained a hint of what might have been taken as genuine concern.

They both stood up. I, unsteadily and slowly, followed suit. I was exhausted but unsure why. I had just woken up only minutes before. As I stood, the earth began a clumsy dance beneath my feet. The short distance to my room felt as though it had, through some occult phenomenon, extended itself by another few hundred yards. While attempting to walk, I had to place my hands on the swaying cinder block walls of the bungalows to try and maintain balance. By the time I finally walked through the doorway of my room a great sense of relief enveloped me. I sat on the end of the bed trying to regain my composure. I was feeling tired, nauseous and antsy all at the same time. If this was what people referred to as "Jet Lag" then I wanted no part of it. I laid back on the bed with my legs hanging over the edge, feet on the cement floor and quickly slid into a hard, uncompromising, vegetative state.

CHAPTER 3

ONE BOWL MANY MOUTHS
eat to live do not live to eat

More than six hours had passed since my collapse. I awoke refreshed, slightly more energized. I was no longer experiencing dizziness and my equilibrium had been restored. The sound of activity, voices and laughter could be heard outside of my room. I didn't like the first impression I had made on my hosts, Bouba and his wife, Momina. I wanted, desperately, to adjust my feelings of social ineptitude and adapt to my surroundings. I looked down and realized that I had fallen asleep with my legs hanging over the edge of the bed. It seemed as if my body had not moved an inch the entire six hours. Sankoun was standing in the doorway. Turning his head left, he yelled something in Mandinka to someone outside and then returned to focus his gaze on me.

"Are you hungry?" he asked excitedly, as if my answer would dictate his opportunity to eat as well.

I silently wondered, "Why are all of my interactions so curt, abrupt?" Maybe it was our obvious language barriers. Maybe everyone was as uncomfortable in their English as I was in my French.

"Yes," I answered.

I was indeed hungrier than I have ever been. A cavern had formed in the pit of my stomach. Once I realized that I had not eaten in twenty-four hours, my hunger pains immediately grew in intensity. The food served on the plane was disgusting and, once again, my clearly defined western sensibilities hadn't permitted me to consider placing it anywhere near my mouth. I was quickly coming to grips with the awareness that, in this setting, my self-proclaimed western sensibilities just might be the death of me.

At the entrance of my tiny bungalow was a small vestibule, an improvised seating area just on the other side of the wall where the bed was. The area had just enough space to house a card table and two white plastic lawn chairs.

"Sit," directed Sankoun, "We will eat."

After about 16 hours in Africa, I had yet to have a full conversation with anyone. I felt as though I was in a perpetual state of receiving instruction: the crew on the plane, the soldiers at the airport and now the family.

Just as Sankoun and I were taking our seats, Momina glided into the room carrying a huge calabash covered with a vibrantly colored piece of fabric. This gourd's circumference was almost the size of the table. The unmistakable aroma of freshly cooked rice filled the room along with something else unfamiliar but equally tantalizing to my sense of smell. She set the calabash down on the table between us and explained, in the most maternal, loving tone, that she hoped I was hungry because she had prepared this dish especially for me.

With those few words my heart felt warm and welcomed. I was experiencing an environment oddly familiar, yet foreign. I was hungry and the task of eating, for the past few days, had not been a priority. Forgetting to eat is an absent-minded pattern I've repeated more often than I care to admit, a very unhealthy one.

A giant cloud of steam climbed the air from beneath the opening of the fabric as she slowly peeled it back.

My stomach turned Pavlovian flips as my eyes soaked in the visual of a long, fat piece of fish. It was covered in a thick red sauce atop a mountainous bed of rice. As my mouth watered at the sight of the food, Momina explained that she had prepared the country's national dish, Ceebu jen, for my first meal in Senegal. She handed me a large spoon and took a step back, standing near the entrance of the room. Sankoun sat at my side. They were both smiling wildly at me.

"Please… eat," pleaded Momina.

I was famished but, for some ungodly reason, my head started a fight with my stomach. Sitting before me was a spread to end all spreads. The contents of the gourd: fish, vegetables, rice, and an incredibly seductive, aromatic sauce. This portion of food was more than any two people, or ten for that matter, could be expected to consume in one sitting. I looked at Momina's smiling face beaming back at me, and I could only return a half-hearted smile. There was an incongruence in the poverty I was witnessing in the surroundings and the banquet that was laid out before me. Something did not feel right about this.

I unpacked my broken French once again and explained to Momina that this was just way too much food.

Before I could speak another word she interrupted with an order, "Manges-tu!" Immediately following the demand, her face returned to its comforting countenance and pleasant smile. This moment was the one and only time that I would experience the ire of this sweet, demure woman. Her command that I eat overflowed with as much love as it did urgency.

Sankoun handed the spoon to me and demanded that I obey her instructions. "Everyone listens to my mother," he explained.

There was no other spoon, and so I offered to share, trying to reciprocate their hospitality. The thought that they couldn't afford another spoon did cross my mind. Sankoun waved me off and said, "I have this!" Ceremoniously, he flung his right hand up in the air before diving wrist deep into the food. He scooped up a fistful of rice and sauce. He had picked off a small portion of the fish and added it to the section of rice and sauce closest to his area of the calabash. He rolled the rice, sauce and fish into a small lump in his fist, squishing and squeezing it as one might do when artistically forming a piece of clay.

I watched in amazement as he shoved the ball of food, along with four fingers, deeply into his mouth. He pushed the food back down his gullet and sucked loudly while pulling the fingers out, slowly, licking in and around each finger as they crossed the border of his lips.

I was as impressed as I was disgusted!

I knew this way of eating to be a cultural norm among many people in most parts of Africa but, in the U.S., none of my friends from the continent had done it with such flare and wantonness.

I didn't want to judge, but I was finding it difficult not to. I had not come to West Africa to be viewed as a foreigner. I watched carefully, studied, as Sankoun took a few more scoops of food into his mouth.

I lifted my right hand as Sankoun had done and dug into the bed of rice. Momina's cheeks puffed with a cook's pride as she smiled. I tried lifting food to my mouth. This skill of eating with your hand was much more complicated than it appeared on the surface. Rice was falling from the sides of my hand; the sauce was dripping from between my fingers. It was a mess! I placed my hand, full of food, into my mouth, fighting my gag reflex and feeling as though I was going to swallow all four of my fingers. However, an involuntary groan of satisfaction escaped me. I slowly pulled my fingers out of my mouth, sucking every last little morsel that could be had. I tilted my head back and closed my eyes, savoring the moment.

My taste buds came alive as I relished the mildly spicy sauce of tomatoes mixed with tiny seeds of unusual spices. The flavor-filled granules dissolved on my tongue within seconds of making contact. Momina had prepared the rice so expertly that each grain appeared to have been cooked individually to flawless precision. The fish was a large, tender, succulent celebration of meat seasoned to perfection.

Momina and Sankoun's laughter shuttled me back to reality. As I opened my eyes, head still tilted back; the ceiling came into focus. I leaned my head forward and pieces of rice fell to the floor. Their uncontrollable laughter had been provoked by the sight of sauce and rice dangling from my nose, forehead and chin. Anyone who claims that eating with your hands is easy has never done it.

Momina beamed, emanating a brilliant, authentic delight that I had witnessed many times growing up down south when my mother, grandmother or great-aunts saw that I was thoroughly enjoying a meal they had prepared. Momina turned without saying a word and walked out of our room. I asked Sankoun if she were going to eat and he curtly responded, "Yes, she will eat."

Sankoun was possibly on his fifth or six mouthful by the time I was reaching for my second. With each handful of deliciousness that I raised toward my lips, I became more and more troubled, uncomfortable, with the enormous amount of food sitting before me. Once again, my mind and stomach were locked in battle.

There was no way that this family could afford to feed me like this today, much less day after day for a couple of months. Guilt weighed heavily on my head. I'm not sure why, but my intuition was telling me that there was something not quite right about this situation.

Sankoun's disposition changed from the serious one I had been experiencing to a lighter, more jovial one as he excitedly engaged me with lots of questions about America. He had a blazing curiosity. He told me that he hoped one day to travel to America. As we were talking, I listened to his perspective on the land of my birth. I began to feel as though he imagined the streets of the United States were paved with gold.

The more I took in my surroundings, while conversing with Sankoun, the more I was plagued by investigative thoughts of how they were able to offer me such an abundance of food. I wasn't trying to be condescending in the least, but the conditions betrayed the level of generosity I was receiving, or thought possible for that matter.

After about my sixth handful I, reluctantly, but with much thought given to the action, pushed my plastic lawn chair back away from the card table and placed my hands over my stomach. Sankoun looked up in surprise.

"You're finished?" he asked, with the most puzzled look on his face, his head tilted sideways.

"Yes, I'm full," I responded. "I can't eat another bite."

I continued massaging my stomach as a gesture to show just how engorged I was feeling... even though I wasn't.

I praised the meal and his mother for having cooked it. Sankoun brusquely stood up, his plastic chair loudly scrapping against the cement floor. He seemed miffed with me.

"You're finished?" he asked once again, in a tone of complete and utter shock.

He finished his last handful while standing and then walked out of the room. Within seconds, he returned with Momina in tow.

"He's finished," Sankoun explained in a tone bordering on anger, pointing at the calabash still filled to the brim with food. Remaining in the gourd was roughly 95% of all that Momina had initially served us.

She gasped loudly and asked me what was wrong! I

motioned for her like I had with Sankoun, rubbing my belly and explaining that I was full.

"Are you sure you are no longer hungry?" she asked me in a hushed, but concerned, tone.

Once again, I patted my stomach and praised her culinary skills to the high heavens. I must have been convincing because her smile radiated a satisfaction that could only come with knowing the truth. She placed the beautiful piece of cloth over the huge calabash and lifted it from the table. Momina instructed me to stay in the room, relax some more so that I would not become sick. Her over-whelming maternal nature had a way of making me feel at home.

She and Sankoun exited the room together with her carry-ing the calabash. I waited a few seconds and then, I'm not sure why I did this but, I followed them. My actions hadn't been part of a plan or anything. In a purely impromptu moment, I found myself walking behind them at a short distance. Neither of them looked back as they began speak-ing Wolof to one another. Their family was Mandinka in origin, having come from the Cassamance region of Sene-gal, but Wolof was the national language. I later learned that everyone in the family spoke more than two or three languages.

They were too engrossed in talking to notice me following them. She and her son walked down the narrow corridor of the compound toward the front gate. Instead of exiting the gate, they turned left into the concrete, open-air common area that I had seen the previous night. Momina was still cupping the calabash as they disappeared from my sight turning the corner.

My stomach cursed my head's propensity for over-thinking as it grumbled loudly, begging for a bit more of the tasty Ceebu Jan.

As I approached the area, the sound of voices grew louder. I didn't even know what I was looking for or expecting to find. I may not have been thinking at all. I turned the corner that Sankoun and Momina had vanished around only seconds before and stopped abruptly, unable to move my feet another step.

There were about 20 people squatting down forming a tight circle, all on their haunches, all barefoot. Momina stepped over their hunched-over bodies and into the center. She then placed the calabash she had just taken from my room down on the ground, lifted the cloth and stepped back over the circular throng of bodies. As she was stepping back out over the circle, she noticed me. She flashed that motherly, entreating smile that was quickly becoming an anchor for my experience.

I stood there gawking at a mass of arms, hands and elbows swinging rapidly back and forth between the gourd and surrounding faces. They were ravenous. They were all yanking out large fistfuls of food, squishing, squeezing, and then shoving their entire hands into their mouths. The multiplied sucking and slurping sounds were much louder and more intense than what I had experienced with Sankoun only moments before.

Due to my experiencing a paralysis of cultural shock at the scene playing out before me, I barely noticed Momina walking by and exiting. I stood there with my mouth agape, staring at what, to me, was an astonishing display. I felt as if I were watching some sort of foreign film or documentary. It was surreal to witness this mass of young men, women and children attack the calabash of rice and fish with such reckless abandon. Within seconds the entire calabash had been emptied of its contents.

As I watched, the crowd began to rise and stand, all sucking on the leftovers on their fingers.

I was experiencing an affirming awareness from having allowed my inner-voice to guide me. I sensed that I had, somehow, contributed instead of taking away from my new surroundings. Over the months of my visit, I would experience this loving level of hospitality from many people in this community, people to whom I was a stranger.

CHAPTER 4

Eaten Alive

one day of disease will destroy a year of health

Being a creature of habit, I sought to establish a routine for myself. Although Bouba kept his distance and didn't talk much, the rest of the family embraced me with open arms, following Momina's model of unconditional love. There was Shariffe, a man close to my age, if not older. He shared one of the single room bungalows with his young wife. Sankoun, although about fifteen years younger than me, became a stern task master during my instructional time learning to play the kora. Moussa, the next oldest brother, acted as a surrogate teacher whenever Sankoun was called away to perform and earn money for the compound. The youngest brother of the family was Sajo, a boy whose warm countenance and easy going demeanor mimicked his mother, Momina's. The jewel of the compound was Sira, Badialy's only sister. She was in her early twenties and exuded an innocence, charm, and beauty that was natural, never forced.

I had come, not as a vacationer, but as a student. I carried a small, portable tape-recorder with me everywhere I went. I didn't want to miss a thing. I was learning language, music, history, and customs. Also, it seemed that each minute of the day, everywhere I turned, I was introduced to someone new. Elders, young men and women, and even chil-

33

dren thought nothing of interrupting whatever I was doing to have me greet a friend or relative of theirs. The role of minor celebrity, "The Black-American," was becoming increasingly burdensome and distracting in my pursuit of knowledge.

About the second, or third night, after my arrival in Senegal, following a torrential afternoon of rain, I was sitting on the ground leaning with my back against my bungalow's wall practicing kora. I looked up and noticed thick, dark miniature clouds forming just above the area near the eaves of the tin roof. It was the strangest thing to watch as these transparent black clouds grew thicker and thicker while appearing to shift and bounce around on air. The night was falling quickly and soon it would be hard to see these little dancing nebulas. I sat surrounded by a group of young men, all pelting me with questions about America. I asked Sajo, Bouba's youngest son, about the little clouds. He laughed from deep in the gut at my ignorance and informed me, "Mosquitoes, you don't know mosquitoes in America?"

In Africa, mosquitoes are known to kill and spread disease. It was frightening to see this cloud of mosquitoes growing thicker and thicker with the lessening of light in the sky.

Everyone, except me of course, knew what was going on. Sajo left my side and returned with a large metal coffee can full of burning coal and wood chips. He started explaining to me how the mosquitoes did not like smoke and the more we burned, the fewer we would have in the compound. I was half-heartedly listening. My mind immediately rushed to the thought that fumes and smoke from coals and burning bark would create a deadly carcinogenic cocktail. Smoke was everywhere!

There must have been about eight young people walking throughout the compound carrying similar cans and placing them on the ground near entrances. The result of this was that the entire compound became shrouded in a thick, choking gray smoke.

I began hacking and coughing. Everyone not placing cans of smoke in doorways continued on as usual, chatting, laughing. I seemed to be the only person affected.

There wasn't a single person who seemed to understand the health dangers we were subjecting ourselves to by inhaling this smoke. I knew much better than everyone the danger of what we were breathing in. I flatly refused to allow the cancer causing smog into my bungalow. I ran to my room and slammed the door and window shut. I had visions of dying in my sleep from smoke inhalation or being poisoned by deadly fumes.

That evening when I went to bed, I made sure to keep the door and window of the bungalow closed. Sankoun was already asleep. When I turned off the lights and got into bed, there was a loud, high-pitched whining buzz slowly filling the room. This noise was totally unfamiliar to me. As I laid there in bed, the high-pitched buzzing grew louder and louder until I felt something whiz past my ear. It was the mosquitoes! There was one whizzing past one ear and then another on the other side of my head. I instinctively slapped at the air but made contact with nothing.

These mosquitoes were aggressive. I felt clumps of them landing on my forehead. I smacked myself hard with an open hand. I then retreated under the covers reasoning that they could not get through the blanket.

I was correct in assuming that they couldn't get through the blanket, but what I had not considered was that I was trapped beneath the thick fabric and had to contend with the lack of air as well as the intense heat.

I waited, anticipating their departure when they could not find a meal. The buzzing quieted, and I felt safe enough to resurface. When I brought my head out from under the covers, the loud buzzing resumed. At first, they buzzed from afar in the room but continued tightening their circle until they were within striking distance of my exposed head.

The interplay between covering up for protection, the mosquitoes going silent, uncovering to breathe and attacks continued for far too long. It was maddening.

These vicious flying leeches had driven me to an intensity of anger that left me unhinged. I decided that I would make it my mission to kill each and every one of them. In a rage, I threw off the covers and turned on the lights. They were all over the place! There must have been thousands of them. I picked up one of my sandals and began smashing it against the ones clinging to the walls. For those that dared to fly, I clapped my hands together to crush them mid-air.

After I had killed a hundred, two hundred more came out of the cracks and crevices of the walls to replace them. I was getting stung, mostly on my back, neck and arms. These weren't the pricks of normal mosquitoes. In the United States, mosquitos didn't sting like wasps.

They were beginning to overwhelm me. There were just too many. My swinging and swatting only made them more aggressive; it was an exercise in futility. They had me beating myself up with forceful slaps trying to keep them at bay. Visually, I was in the throes of a mad man's dance of self-torture.

I began a foul mouth rant, cursing these evil parasites in a manner I never knew I was capable. In desperation, I ran outside and retrieved one of the little burning coffee cans of toxicity. I brought the can back into my room and slammed the door shut. Sure enough, the little bleeders scattered. I made sure that smoke filled every square inch of the space.

The fumes were caustic. I gasped and choked from the combination of burning coal and bark. I placed the can on the floor near the closed entrance and was satisfied that I had triumphed.

I looked over at Sankoun, and he was laying there, sleeping so peacefully. Nothing that had just occurred moved him or disturbed his sleep.

I crawled back under the blanket and quickly fell into slumber. I'm not sure how long I managed to sleep, but a burning, stinging sensation on my feet shot me awake. The loud buzzing was back! The can of coal and bark had burned itself out, and the mosquitoes had strategically lain in wait. My feet and ankles were immersed in flames that I could not douse.

I threw off the blankets and began slapping at my feet. I could feel each bite.

I spent the rest of the night jumping in and out of bed, turning off and on lights, smashing mosquitoes with my hands, burning coals and wood chips, falling asleep, being awakened by searing, painful bites and then… starting the dance of madness all over again. By this time, they had settled on my feet, ankles and legs as the most delectable portions of my body.

During the night, looking over at Sankoun only made me angry. How was he able to sleep so peacefully while I was being eaten alive? Why weren't they biting and stinging him?

I crawled back into bed only to have to jump back out minutes later. I covered myself with the blanket and thought seriously of suffocation as an alternative to the torture. I dozed and awoke time and time again until it reached the point that I could no longer fight. I could no longer keep my eyes open. I passed out, surrendering my body to the blood suckers to do with whatever they wanted.

I felt the grip of someone's hand on my shoulder shaking me.

"Baba wake up!"

It was Sankoun trying to wake me for our morning lesson. I wiped and opened my eyes and could see that the sun was high in the sky. The light was filtering throughout closed shutters and cracks around the door.

Sankoun and I had established a routine. We would practice for three sessions each day for about an hour. The rest of the day I would spend practicing what I had learned.

My face must have registered contempt and anger because Sankoun stepped away from me. I glared at him as if he had caused the evening's misery. While I fought throughout the night for my life, he had lain there like a swaddled baby. None of the noise during the night had even caused him to stir, and now here he was standing over me, shaking me awake.

I gained my composure and was able to assume a mask of pleasantry as I raised myself from the dead.

My trip to Africa was not working out to be the romanticized reunion of souls that I had envisioned. It seemed each day and night, I was being subjected to conditions threatening my health, life and sanity. The worst part was that my suffering seemed isolated to me. I polled several members of the compound, and no one else had suffered the previous night as I had.

It was an odd juxtaposition of feelings to experience the joy of being surrounded by so many supportive souls and yet haunted by an inexplicable isolation.

I got up, washed and came back into the room. After washing, Sankoun would guide me through my lessons on the kora, first introducing me to a song's kumbengo (ostinato) or a few short notes played over and over again. It would usually take me hours to build up good muscle memory to feel accomplished on each kumbengo, but I was determined. Each time I would master the basics, Sankoun would add more by making it a bit more complicated. By the end of each day, I would almost be playing an entire song.

For me, playing the ancient harp began as a meditative practice, a way of connecting with the past. I wanted to play and manipulate the strings to produce sounds that might have been heard by my ancestors. I wanted to sing a song that might have been sung by relations far removed by time. I had hopes of, eventually, sharing this meditative passion with others. I never dreamed that this desire would one day have me crossing the ocean to learn, but here I was.

Today, it was nearly impossible to keep my hands on the kora because of the need to scratch the itching of my ankles and legs.

After about an hour of learning, we would drink tea and eat bread, a typical breakfast. It was the afternoon meal that everyone looked forward to, the meal in the big calabash.

As much as I was enjoying learning the kora during the day, I dreaded the coming of the evening because it brought with it the black clouds of mosquitoes. I wasn't getting used to it. I was becoming a defeated soul, learning to sacrifice parts of my body to get sleep. I was even getting better at surviving the suffocation beneath the blankets. I slept, but never well, because there always seemed to be a mosquito in the attacking mob that stung harder and deeper than all of the others.

Within a few days, large scabs and puss-filled sores blistered my feet and ankles. Fatigue set in. I was deathly afraid that I had contracted malaria or some other insect-born illness.

The days passed quickly, the nights slowly. Sankoun introduced me to the repertoire of the ancient, oral historians known as griots. He would give me a kumbengo to practice along with an explanation or story associated with the traditional piece.

In the morning, I would lose myself in a narrow funnel of concentration. Conquering the clumsiness of my fingers attempting to play the strings trapped me in a hypnotic state. I knew I was capable but the introduction of each new song was accompanied by feelings of inadequacy and awkwardness. So intense was my focus that I often had to remind myself to breathe.

The only interruptions during the day were when my body fought against me. I would be lost in the incremental successes of achieving the exact sounds the strings were meant to produce when my stomach would begin gnawing on itself. I would have to break to eat. I would achieve a basic dexterity of playing an entire song, which was motivation to continue driving forward, when the pesky needs of my bowels would demand urgent attention.

Approximately seven to nine hours of each day was spent cross legged-seated behind the kora, mastering the simplest of musical phrases.

One of the first pieces that we worked on was called Tiedo or Cheddo. This song chronicles a conflict between the Mandinka people and the Fula people. The Mandinka were dominant, and the Fula felt as though they were living under tyrannical subjugation. Caravaners came from the east, bringing with them the religion of Islam. The Fula people began accepting the new religion in droves and uniting with other populations of Muslims. Over time, an enormous conflict erupted between the two groups. Cheddo is the narrative of that conflict. It is an aggressive song, demanding an assertive style of plucking the kora strings. It was not a comfortable, melodic song for me to play. In fact, Cheddo caused me headaches whenever it had to be practiced.

The heat of Africa is not heat in the common understanding of the word. Many days the earth was a furnace where we were being cooked alive. There was no air conditioning, no escaping the attempted cremation of each day.

I would sit in my room or its doorway in the shade, marinating in sweat. It took every ounce of fortitude I could muster to focus on my lessons. I sat there with the kora cradled between my legs trying to force my fingers to move the way I saw them moving in my mind. Inevitably, the overwhelming urge to scratch at the sores and lesions would force me to stop. The combination of open wounds and salty sweat acted as periodic deterrents. I scratched, burned and then scratched some more. It was a cycle of insanity.

Larger scabs and sores began to form on my feet, ankles and legs. My strength was waning with each passing day. I pushed past the physical pain and fatigue. I brought full focus onto my studies.

At times, my singular concentration alienated me from the routines of the compound. When I was absorbed in my studies, I lost all sense of time.

Momina, with ever watchful eyes, helped keep me grounded. She constantly interrupted my practices, never allowing me to go for too long. She would force me to eat or drink something before permitting me to continue.

Over the next few weeks, Sankoun pushed me to my limits of learning. We went through so many songs within such a short period of time that I would often get light-headed while practicing. Once he saw that I was a capable learner he became insistent that I absorb three or four songs during each instructional session.

One morning I woke exhausted. It was strange. I had slept all night but could no longer remain in bed. It was as if I were too tired to sleep. The intense sessions of learning were beginning to take their toll on my health. Groggily, I walked out into the misty, early morning air and was greeted by Badialy's grandmother, an old woman who had to be in her late eighties, possibly early nineties. She was screaming at me in Mandinka. I could not understand a single word. My inability to communicate heightened her anger. She raged, stomping her feet and spitting on the ground in front of me. Her eyes tore through me with such vitriol and venom that I was scared. She threw a few ignoble hand gestures in the air within inches of my face as she turned her back on me and stormed off into her bungalow.

I stood there confused, frozen by fear, anxiety and anger. There is no appropriate way to defend yourself against an elderly woman.

Bouba walked out of the entrance of he and Momina's bungalow to investigate the commotion. It was quickly becoming a nightmare of an experience. How could I tell Bouba that I had just had some sort of altercation with his mother? My fight or flight response kicked in. I could run, but there was no where to run. I could stand my ground, but what, exactly, would I be fighting for or defending? Confusion peppered my thoughts with chaotic precision.

As Bouba approached me, I must have appeared dazed because he asked me what was going on. I could think of nothing to do but tell the truth and suffer whatever retribution he might enact to defend his mother's cause for attacking me.

His face was stoic the entire time I shared what had just

occurred. Bouba's flat affect and his lack of emotional response was frightening.

Without announcing his intentions, he abruptly walked past me and into his mother's room.

From the moment he disappeared into her bungalow, time stopped. My angst and anxiety created a fear in me that turned a minute into an hour. Trying to anticipate the unknown is torture. I didn't move from the spot he had left me. I felt like a child about to receive punishment for an act not of my own making.

When Bouba exited his mother's room, his face was bright and he was laughing hysterically. This was not a Bouba I had ever seen before. Fear and confusion were my only companions as my heart took residence in my throat.

"She thinks that you are lying to the family about who you are!"

I wasn't understanding. I think he could tell by the look on my face that nothing was making sense to me.

"My mother says that she knows you and your family. She knew you when you were a child. She has told everyone in the compound that you did not come here from America and that you are Peulh. She says that you are here trying to trick all of us and we should be careful."

Doubled over from laughter, Bouba held out his arm against the wall to steady himself. If being the butt of a joke endeared me to Bouba, then I was willing to make the sacrifice. Finally, I felt as though I had broken through his rough veneer.

Laughter is medicinal, and it felt good to see him enjoying himself, even if it was at my expense. He let me know that he had cleared up the issue the with his mother and that she would not be attacking me again.

Bouba returned to his bungalow laughing and slapping at his sides hysterically.

I went back to practicing my kora.

Now, within three weeks of my arrival, the scabs and sores on my legs, ankles and feet were so bad that everyone in the compound was becoming worried.

Although I was feeling frail, my obsessive nature wouldn't allow me to focus on anything but mastering the songs that Sankoun was teaching me.

I coped with the evening mosquitoes by staying up throughout the night, burning the repellent bark and then napping during the day. I would practice, quietly, during these nights. I was surviving, barely, on an average of about 3 to 4 hours of sleep at intervals throughout the day.

Exhaustion and illness were setting in. It reached a point where I would fall asleep in a chair or sitting on the ground leaning against a wall. I began retreating to my room with my kora and trying to practice but, every time I touched the instrument I would slump over and pass out.

One afternoon Bouba was standing over me in my room shaking me awake.

"You will go to Gorée Island," he began, "On Gorée, you will be healed."

Bouba sat down on the floor next to my bed and leaned against the wall. He had a very worried look on his face as he began telling me that he had made arrangements for his sons to escort me to the island.

Due to my semi-conscious state, I wasn't comprehending all of his words, but I understood him to say that something on Gorée would help me feel better. I don't know how long he talked but I sensed the concern in his tone as I drifted in and out of consciousness.

It had long been a dream of mine to one day visit the island of Gorée, especially the infamous "Doorway of No Return."

Deeply submerged in the shadowy isolation of my own mind, I doubted I would ever see the island, or the U.S. again for that matter. I was experiencing dreamy loosely formed thoughts of death as a welcome relief. Somewhere between semi-consciousness and sleep I found comfort in the potential of dying. Had my ancestors brought me back to Africa to die so that their souls could finally be at peace?

CHAPTER 5

THE BLIND HARPIST

the sky is no less blue for the blind

Time in Africa is elastic, like winds of the Sahel, it bends, twists and molds itself into impermanent shapes. My trip to Gorée did not happen right away, not even days later. I was beginning to understand that "soon" in Africa was an abstraction that could mean today, tomorrow or maybe even some time in the distant future. When Bouba had told me that his sons would be taking me to the island and that my healing would commence there, I had an unwavering faith in his words. Even though he had shared the least amount of time, and spoken the fewest words with me, I felt as though he were an all-knowing, beneficent being.

Over the next few days I could not muster the will to practice the kora. I was getting weaker. I was in no condition to do anything physical. Whenever I attempted to sit up, stand or walk, my body would force me back down onto my bed. In spite of my weakened state, nothing deterred the constant throng of inquisitive visitors from entering my room unannounced. I was an aberration in the small town of Thiaroye. One prevailing theme in all of the conversations with my guests was that they had never known, or met, a "Black-American" before.

Because I wasn't taking lessons or studying, Sankoun soon

disappeared. I didn't know where he was going each day, or what he was up to, but he always seemed overly busy, rushed even. Each night he would return, take his side of the bed and set world records for falling asleep faster than any other human being on the planet. My irrational disdain for him and his ability to sleep though the chaos of the compound was truly more envy than anything else.

I was now spending each day and night trapped in my bed, unable to find the strength to even sit up. After about three days and four nights, I sensed Momina becoming increasingly alarmed. One time, she came into my room carrying a clinking glass. Ice! This was an incredible feat because there was nothing cold or ice producing anywhere near the compound. Due to the incredible heat of each day, it would be impossible for someone to come from a distance carrying ice. Ice melted within seconds when exposed to the hot African air. It was nothing short of a miracle.

Momina held a vigil over me, repeating long prayers in Arabic and chanting in whispered tones. Most of the time she sat with her eyes closed while rocking back and forth in one of the white plastic lawn chairs placed next to my bed. Even though she had very little command of English, she and I communicated effectively. Whenever Momina wasn't speaking, her eyes had the unique ability to articulate what was in her heart. I would wake to see her sitting there and then, moments later, fall back asleep.

As insane as it might seem, I felt safe in this family's care and wasn't in fear of my circumstances. I was trusting the Cissoko family with my body and soul. Bouba's strong paternal nature combined with Momina's nurturing spirit elicited a familiar, childlike comfort in me. There was also a part of me that had faith in my own body to heal itself.

I had never been one to take medications of any type. All of my life I had been reasonably healthy, never this sick. I continued a mantra telling myself that things would be better soon.

I let her know that she didn't have to sit there with me all the time. I told her that I was doing well and feeling stronger with each passing hour. She offered me a weak smile. She knew that I was not an accomplished liar.

I woke one morning and my eyes were itching, burning fiercely. I could not stop the continuous need to rub deep into the sockets of my eyes. When Momina came into the room with my tea and bread, she gasped loudly, quickly turned and ran out in a panic. I wasn't sure what was going on until she returned with Bouba. Bouba's long, dread ridden face told me everything that I needed to know. Something was terribly wrong.

In that moment, I realized that I had not looked into a mirror since my arrival. There were no mirrors anywhere in the compound. I wanted to know what it was that they were seeing. The disconcerting expressions on their faces were starting to cause me concern.

Bouba asked me if I had been shaking hands "American-style" with everyone who had come to visit me. Unable to keep my hands from rubbing my eyes I answered yes. He sighed deeply. While scratching my eyes, I started to feel a flood of fluid all over my fingers. It was thick with a milky constancy, but transparent. The more I rubbed my eyes; the more goo oozed out onto my hands.

"Stop that!" commanded Bouba, "You must not put your hands in your eyes!"

The itching was so freakishly fierce that there wasn't anyone, including him, that was going to stop me. The more I
rubbed, the more it itched but I couldn't control myself, I
couldn't stop. The only thing that halted me from digging
my entire fist into my eye sockets to gain relief was Bouba
shouting at the top of his lungs, "You will be blind if you
don't stop that now!"

Although the compulsion to continue digging into my eyes
had possession of me, the reality of Bouba's words made
me stop. A million questions scrambled through my mind.
What did I have? What had happened? Had the mosquitoes
caused this? Was I going blind? I was rapidly declining
into a panic. The safety I felt before was quickly fading.
Momina began sobbing with her face planted deeply into
her hands, walking around in frenzied circles. Bouba had
his sons take their mother out of the room and then barked
orders at one of the young men standing around outside
of my bungalow. Four weeks into this journey and I had
already been subjected to a lifetime's worth of experiences.
There was a crowd assembled outside of my room in the
doorway, peering through the window. He returned to my
bedside and said, "We are going to get you medicine."

Bouba explained that what I had was common and that
many people were suffering from this malady since the
last rains had come. He assured me that "most" people
recovered from this after a few days. The word "most"
slapped me in the face. The word echoed off of the walls
of my room. Bouba sat there next to my bed repeating the
command that I do not rub my eyes anymore. "It will get
worse."

The feeling started as a simple itch needing to be scratched
but the more I resisted, the more intense the sensation

became until finally it would begin to feel as though I had tiny creatures with spindly, stringy legs racing across my eyeballs and into the corners of my eyes. Reflexively, I drew my hands towards my face, Bouba grabbed them.

"No!" he barked, "You cannot do this!"

The itching was so monstrously severe that I considered punching Bouba in the face to get a few rubs into my eye sockets before he could recover. I don't know how I did it, but I kept my hands away from my eyes.

Sajo, Bouba's youngest son, came into the room with a big calabash of water and a towel. Bouba began dipping the towel and soaking my eyes with the water as he wrung the rag over my face. Water was falling everywhere, down my cheeks, all over the blankets. It didn't matter because I was experiencing the most soothing relief. The water felt like cascading sheets of cooling solace. When the water would finish streaming down my face, the agitating itching would return immediately with a vengeance. I felt like I needed someone to just continue pouring water over my face nonstop so that I could maintain that soothing feeling. A few times I drifted off into a fantasy of sticking my head into a bucket of cold water and ice, submerging my head and opening my eyes wide. The thought of this made me swoon.

Bouba kept the cycle of wringing the rag over my face going for a good 20 minutes. I had lain there with my eyes closed. When I opened my eyes, everything was blurry, and the itching ensued with much greater fervor. A milky film formed over my cornea that would not go away. Each time I opened my eyes, things became progressively more blurry. I could make out figures, large objects, and some colors but that was about it.

The young man Bouba had ordered to go and get the medicine returned; he came running into the room, panting, out of breath. He handed Bouba something, but I could not see what it was.

"Here," Bouba commanded once again, "You drink!"

He pulled my hand up from my side and placed, what felt like, four pills in it. Instant agitation and fear took hold of me. I didn't take medications of any type, I never had and I swore that I never would. I was worried. I had no idea what it was that Bouba was trying to give me. If I swallowed this stuff, what would happen to me? A burning sensation was churning up in my eyes and the irritation was becoming more than I could handle. The sores on my legs, ankles and feet were starting to burn as well, but that was weak in comparison to the searing flames melting my eyeballs. Out of desperation, I cupped the pills and threw them all into my mouth at once. I then chased them down with as much water as I could ingest.

I may never know the series of events that followed because everything, everyone around me slowed and appeared a blurred haze of strange colors, shapes and forms. Within minutes of taking the pills that Bouba had given me, I began drifting off towards unconsciousness. It felt almost like what happens when an anesthesiologist places a mask over your face and tells you to count backward from one hundred. I might have only made it to ninety-three before darkness swept over me.

At one point, as I was drifting off, my eyes tightly shut,

my ears were deciphering the sounds of a solemnly moving parade of people entering and exiting my room. No one was speaking English, only Wolof, Peuhl or Mandinka. The procession of people walking in and out of my room reminded me of mourners walking by a casket of a loved one during a viewing of the body. But I wasn't dead! I floated between states of semi-consciousness and unconsciousness. There was a low level of conflict between my body and mind. My body would feel restless as my head attempted to lull it into inactivity. Other times my head engaged a frenetic pace of thoughts while my body felt lifeless. I couldn't say how long it took but, eventually, my mind and body coalesced into a deep sleep.

The time that had elapsed seemed miniscule. It felt as if only a few minutes had passed. When I finally woke, I tried to open my eyes but could not. I panicked. My eyes had been glued shut! I reached up and felt a flaky crust covering them. No matter how hard I tried I could not open my eyes. Confusion set in and fear overtook me as I yelled out a string of unintelligible words. What I didn't know was that my room was already packed with people, Bouba and Momina being closest to my bed. I felt a set of rough, calloused hands sliding under my back and over my head, lifting my torso. I was helped up into a sitting position on my bed.

"You need to drink," explained Bouba as I felt a small plastic cup being pushed into my hands. Once again, cold water. I guzzled the cup of water like a man rescued from the desert. While it felt good going down, the burning, aching sensation it caused in my stomach forced me to wretch a bit and my chest to tighten.

I couldn't sit up for too long without feeling myself weakening. The longer I sat upright, the more I felt my vitality slipping away. Bouba, once again, positioned his hands on my back and over my heart, supporting me and helping me ease into a reclining position.

As I was being lowered back down onto the bed, I remember saying over and over again, "Bouba I can't see... I can't see!" My heart's palpitations had to have been jumping at over 200 beats per minute. My chest was on the verge of exploding. "My eyes... I can't see... I can't see!"

This pendulum of psychological and physical distress was becoming more than I could bear. At one point death seemed a welcome, comforting companion but now potential blindness was sending me into a panic. I was a fool. There was no one to blame for my current state but me. I had placed my faith on the tenuous idea of Africa as a place of spiritual enlightenment. Only an idiot would purposefully place themselves in harm's way. Was the very foundation of my identity constructed upon a fallacy? Fear was directing my thoughts.

I don't know how he did it, but Bouba managed to calm me down long enough to explain that I had been asleep for two days and that the trouble with my eyes was temporary. He sifted through my leavening hysteria and let me know that he had applied a medicinal cream over my eye lids. The crust that was hardening and flaking was the ointment drying. My condition, I learned much later, had been a combination of malaria, dehydration, and a severe form of conjunctivitis. Bouba had given me pills meant to fight the malaria and lack of sleep. They were only supposed to help me rest for a few hours, but my body, not used to taking medications, combined with a compromised immune system, caused a two-day absence from the living.

Bouba spoke with such confidence that I innately understood him to know what he was talking about. I had come ill-prepared and was paying a heavy price for my ignorance.

Bouba had me stand, which was difficult, but I managed to get to my feet. I was weak and needed to reorient my body to being upright. In addition to the two days of sleep, I had been in bed for more than five days. My blood began to reach my feet and legs. The natural balance of my body was slowing returning. The children of the compound took turns escorting me around, keeping me walking. I must have been a sight to see. I was dressed in an ankle-length tunic, nothing else, and had a stick to help me whenever I felt weak or my equilibrium faltered.

Although weak, I returned to practicing the kora. I still could not see but there was something therapeutic in sitting for hours allowing my fingers to glide slowly over the 21 nylon strings. Not being able to use my eyes elevated the tactile experience of playing the instrument. This was one of the few things that brought me joy. My youthful, romanticized visions of Africa had become opaque apparitions, slowly fading away with the light of each day, like dreams. I became responsible for rubbing the medicinal cream into my own eyes. Eventually its crust thickened so much that it extended out from my eyelids and caked over my entire socket area. The dense crust began to crackle and fall away itself. By the third day of my blindness, I was back to opening my eyes and was restored to making out blurry patterns and figures.

I stopped applying the creme and, by the seventh day, my eyesight had cleared up entirely. I was weak, but whole again, minus the scabs and sores on my feet and legs. The mosquitoes were no longer attacking me during the night. No matter how much I exposed my skin to them during the evening, they were turning their collective noses up at me as a meal. Maybe because I was extremely sick, or because my body had accumulated a high level of toxins. I could have slept totally nude and not a single mosquito would have dared to venture near me. It seemed that the temporary pleasure they might have gained by feasting on me was tempered by their need for self-preservation.

My blindness had propelled me forward in my learning. The physical dependence that had become necessary for me to navigate my environment enabled me to approach my harp from a more intimate vantage point. My hands were becoming increasingly adept at jumping around the strings without having to rely on my eyes.

Learning the songs became even more exciting. Hearing the stories of history was intriguing. I realized I was no longer in conflict with my surroundings. The poverty that had been so repellent when I arrived was giving way to a discovery of the true beauty around me. I wasn't feeling any stronger physically, but my mind was experiencing a renaissance of its own. I found myself growing more and more comfortable in the compound, not desiring to venture out beyond the massive metal gates. The morning tea and bread became a delicacy I looked forward to. My meals, eaten out of the calabash, became a welcome interruption to my practicing the kora. At night I would smile when I heard the buzzing of the mosquitoes knowing that they didn't want any part of me. If I could maintain the course that I was on, staying close to the compound, practicing my kora and learning from the many who visited, then my body would surely have time to become healthy once again.

One morning, after I had become comfortably ensconced in my routine and the rhythm of the compound, Bouba came into my room and announced, "Today, you go to Gorée!"

CHAPTER 6

SUICIDAL LEAP

the strength of the heart is born from faith

I was finally leaving for the island of Gorée. It was early in the morning. Bouba's sons, Sankoun, Moussa, Sajo and three other young men were charged with escorting me. Due to the previous uncontrollable clawing at my feet, they had become a swollen topography of blood-dried scabs, sores and puss-filled indentations. While they had not been a focus during my illness they now drew my attention.

Sankoun and I, his two brothers and the other three young men caught a taxi on one of the main roads not far from the compound. Our over-packed taxi headed across town from Thiaroye to the coastal port in Dakar to catch the ferry to Gorée Island. I was still weak and, except for the damage done to my skin by the mosquitoes, starting to experience the power of hope. I was looking forward to this magical cure that was some giant secret they wouldn't share. I was saying and doing things that I would never have thought of saying or doing back in the states. Following the instructions of boys much younger than me and trusting and believing in the journey. This mode of functioning was unsettling, and difficult, but felt necessary. I was in a land entirely unfamiliar to me, but proud of my growing ability to adapt. I had come to Africa with preconceived notions of what I needed, what I would learn and a desire to dictate direction. I was quickly becoming aware that such levels of control are often illusions.

In spite of, or maybe because of, the trials I was experiencing, I was becoming more aware of myself both mentally and spiritually.

My desire had been to reconnect to the souls of my ancestors. I didn't know how, or even if such a thing were possible. I was adrift, moving on faith, intuition, and blind trust. In my mind, was an imaginary map of the places the feet of my ancestors might have trodden; if not them, then those whose experiences had been the same. I wanted to walk in the path of my ancestors. The island of Gorée had presented itself to me as a place of pilgrimage, which would allow me to do just that. I had first heard of its "House of Slaves" and the infamous "Doorway of No Return" and sensed a connection might be made there.

The island is a memorial, a living memory of one of the most horrific periods in human history, the Trans-Atlantic Slave Trade. From the 15th to the 19th Century it was the largest center of trafficking in human souls along the West African Coast. It's estimated that more than 20 million men, women, and children might have passed through the island of Gorée onto their final destinations in The Americas.

My main point of interest on Gorée was the House of Slaves built around 1776 by the Dutch. Beneath the main house are cells where the unfortunate captives were crammed together, men and women separated. From these cells, there is a narrow passage that leads out through a single doorway that meets the Atlantic Ocean. It is believed that this was one of the final points of debarkation, the last piece of Africa many of the enslaved might have experienced before suffering the three-month journey to the Americas aboard slave ships.

We arrived at the ticketing office for the ferry to Gorée. The young woman behind the gated window pointed at me. I was standing behind Sankoun, in a crowd of the other young men. She asked him a question in Wolof. Although I couldn't understand a single word, I was immediately put off by her demeanor. It was dismissive, offensive to me and I wasn't getting a good feeling at all. Sankoun began arguing with the young woman, waving his hands around in the air.

Each time the young woman spoke emphatically to Sankoun she would look over his shoulder at me. Other people in the line behind him would turn and look my way as well. Not having command of the language in another land is disconcerting. Each time she looked from the window over Sankoun's shoulder, I felt her disdain. I was becoming angry but I didn't know why. She was upsetting Sankoun and so my empathic response was to be upset as well. On top of this, our little group was attracting quite a bit of attention.

Sankoun left the ticketing window in a huff and pulled me aside. I asked him what was going on, and he brushed me off by saying, "It's nothing Baba... don't worry." He needed the money to secure the tickets for us to board the ferry. I had already known that it was my responsibility to pay for everyone's transportation and this wasn't a surprise. The surprise came when he told me how much he needed and, it was at this point that I discovered why he had been arguing with the young woman. He needed 30 French Francs from me, 15 more than for everyone else in our party. I must have had a look of complete confusion on my face as I eyed Sankoun. I pointed at the sign above the ticketing window which was almost half that amount.

"No Baba, for you, it will be 30 Francs," he insisted.

At the time this was equivalent to maybe $7 or $9 US Dollars.

My head was a spinning ball of confusion. I needed him to explain, clearly, what was happening. He then directed my attention to the sign over the ticketing gate that read, "Europeans – 30 Francs."

"European?" I yelled. "European? The girl thinks I am European?"

Sankoun's demeanor became humbler as he requested, "Please Baba, do not cause problems here. It will make much trouble for us."

I was now more perplexed than confused and becoming angry. Why would I have to pay the same price as someone from Europe?

I went to the ticketing window to speak to the young woman, but she spoke no English. Sankoun stood off in the distance, away from me. I forced him over to translate. I explained that I was not European and that I shouldn't have to pay anything considering it was "my" ancestors who had been forcefully taken from here.

I was incredulous and, by now, on fire! I went on a rant that should have had the police called. I was livid. I aggressively admonished her.

"How dare you try and charge me more!" I bellowed. "My ancestors already paid the ultimate price!"

She was indifferent, sucking her teeth and rolling her eyes.

That sent me reeling into a whole other dimension of anger and resentment. I went on a rant so crazed that I knew Sankoun was not keeping up with me to translate my words.

I think I went on for 3 to 5 more minutes when Moussa, Sankoun, Sajo and the three other young men grabbed me and pulled me away from the ticketing window. I was fighting and struggling against them continuing to spit my vitriolic recitations in the direction of the young woman behind the window. There was nothing rational in my heightened state of anger. It was an erupting volcano of pent-up emotion.

What should have been a simple transaction became symbolic of an exploitation of one African over another. My anger was steeped in the violation of a soul's right to be at peace. I was on a spiritual mission being hijacked by evil. I was honoring "our" ancestors but required to pay more to do so!

The young men had me surrounded and had pushed me down to the pavement onto my butt. "Baba please!" they pleaded.

Sajo was rubbing my back and shoulders. I began to curse the thought of ever having come to Senegal. I began to simmer in a pot of self-pity and anger. Being seen as anything other than a fellow African was nothing short of blunt force trauma to my psyche. The anger that boiled up from the pain in my heart was the raw feeling of rejection. I was seething. Sankoun's calming gentle voice managed to push through the waves of agitation that had closed me off to the world.

Nothing in Africa ever seemed to come with ease. At every corner of every turn, I was being challenged or thrown into struggles. I sat there on the ground listening to Sankoun try and reason with me in a very mature manner. My thoughts swirled aimlessly between listening with focus and beating myself up for having unrealistic, romanticized notions of what Africa would be like. Sankoun's persuasive speech eventually managed to strike a resonant chord. I, reluctantly, handed him the money for the tickets. As I released my grip on the money, I felt a churning of acidic fluid burning in my stomach, making its way up into my throat.

Sankoun went back to the window to purchase our tickets while I sat on the ground, seething. There was no consoling me. I had come thousands of miles as an "African-American" on a spiritual quest, only to be looked at as a "European". I had never hated another human being in my life, but that young girl behind the gated ticketing window became, for me, the personification of those soulless beings who sold their brothers and sisters into bondage.

Sankoun returned with the tickets. The mood was somber. My disposition was infecting everyone present. We were all sullen as we eventually boarded the ferry to Gorée. My anger would not subside. Once we were well under way, the young men tried joking around in front of me, acting like clowns at times. Normally, I would have imbibed the clean sea air, but nothing was pulling me out of my self-imposed angst.

The boat ride across the waters was a reminder for me of the path many of my ancestors had taken. The smell of the salty sea air, the rocking of the ferry and the view of the mainland shores slowly moving away from us set my active imagination in motion. It was as it had been before. No one, except me, was experiencing the familiarity, the parallels of the past.

Where was the calm demeanor I typically carried with me in the States? What had happened to the rational, well-read being I had always thought myself to be?

Sankoun, his brothers, and the other boys gave up entertaining me once they spotted a few young girls familiar to them seated on the other side of the ferry. This was the one moment on the ride to the island that made me smile. Regardless of culture, ethnicity or religious affiliation, proximity to the female form has the universal capacity to distract even the most singularly minded men.

As we neared Gorée Island, the anger I had experienced on Dakar's docks began to dissipate. I thought to myself, "Am I going to allow that young girl behind the ticketing gates to ruin my experience?" The anticipation of setting foot on the island countered my blue mood. Visiting Gorée had long been a dream of mine. Other than learning the music and stories of griots, this was one of the primary reasons for my trip to Senegal. However, my sickness and other problems had troubled me so much that the idea of visiting the island had become nothing more than an illusive dream.

Once we disembarked, with urgency, we quickly separated from the throng of tourists and visitors. I had become accustomed to their laissez-faire demeanors and was thrown off balance by the abrupt change in behavior. Sankoun directed the pack and led us to another side of the island, a bit more deserted. We must have walked for about twenty or thirty minutes. It was beautiful and lush with green vegetation.

We were navigating brush and hanging vines along a path high above the shores. I asked Sankoun if this were the way to the House of Slaves. It wasn't, and he made sure that I knew Bouba had given them instructions to take me to this place first.

He was purposely cryptic, and I hated it. Everyone seemed to enjoy secrets and things of a clandestine nature. I felt like most people I was encountering were controlling me by offering as little information as possible. We dipped and climbed along a winding path of trees, large bushes and dirt until we came to an area of enchantment; a view so spectacular that it warmly hugged my soul. We had emerged from a small wooded area of brush and trees and were now standing on the edge of a small cliff, about 40 feet above the ocean.

My love affair with the majestic view took an unanticipated turn. Sankoun looked over at me and then pointed, "You go, you jump Baba!"

What?

He wanted me to jump off of this cliff? A barrage of demeaning names for him was balancing on the tip of my tongue. He shook his head in negation at me and began to clarify.

"Bouba told me you would say no, Baba. He also told me

to tell you that you are not in America any longer. If you want to feel better, you "must" jump."

There was never a moment for grounding myself, for catching my breath or time to be in my own head for extended periods without interruption. I seemed to be going from one traumatic, or death inviting experience to the next. Was the universe conspiring against me, with me, or for me?

Sankoun's brothers, Moussa, and Sajo as well as the other young men crowded around me on the edge of the cliff and began entreating me to jump. They shared tales of others who had come to this spot and received healing after jumping. They vigorously encouraged me.

I cautiously walked to the edge and leaned forward to look out over the side of the cliff. Below was the Atlantic Ocean!

As we stood there, they allowed me a few minutes to think, which felt like a luxury. I chose to relax into the moment. It seemed that, up to this point, I had continually been struggling against everyone, everything, including myself. I chose to accept this moment for what it was, a new and unknown variable dropped across my life's path. I could struggle against it or acknowledge it was there. I could choose to go over, around, or through it.

I looked up at the young men from my introspective conference and just smiled. I was at peace with whatever might be ahead of me. Without saying a word, I turned and stripped down out of "all" of my clothing.

"Baba, you cannot do that, you must wear something!" Sankoun yelled excitedly.

I didn't say a word. The other three young men gathered to retrieve my tunic as I discarded it. Moussa stood there with the most perplexed expression on his face. Without warning them, naked, I started sprinting toward the edge of the cliff. I must have run about twenty or thirty steps before leaping up and over the side. I had pushed off from the side of the cliff with one of my feet to propel myself as far out toward the sea as possible, as far away from land as I could go. My heart turned somersaults, ending up in my throat and all of the organs of my body felt as though they were departing from me in different directions. It was only a few seconds, but there was a feeling of eternity passing as my body met the air. I was falling into the awaiting arms of the Atlantic Ocean.

The chilling shock of the icy waters pulling me under seeped into my bones. The threat of hypothermia was instantaneous, but fleeting. For a few seconds, as I was going under, I felt shrouded, insulated from the rest of the world and the world's troubles. I allowed myself to sink deep into the shadowy depths. Holding my breath deeply, I looked up and opened my eyes. The deeper I sank, the colder it got. The rays of the sun grew dimmer. My sense of survival kicked in as I, aggressively, swam toward the sun. When my head crowned the water's surface, an unparalleled exhilaration had taken ahold of me.

I floated there on my back, allowing the waves to bounce gently and rock me, as the Atlantic cradled me. From that vantage point, everything around me seemed a miracle. Seagulls flew overhead and off in the distance were fishermen in old dugout canoes.

Still standing above me, on the cliff were Sankoun, his brothers, and the other young men. The looks on their faces betrayed their outward cheer for me. I could see that they were concerned.

I yelled up to them, "Come in! Jump!"

My maniacal, taunting laughter that followed must have given them just the encouragement they needed. Each of them, except Sankoun, jumped from the cliff into the waters below.

I must have stayed out in that ocean for more than an hour, floating, back-stroking, and swimming to my heart's content. I was feeling re-energized. I hadn't felt such vigor since arriving in Senegal! Around the edge of the cliff, not too far up the shore, was a small secluded beach. I hadn't noticed it during my leap of faith but, it was there within swimming distance. I followed the shoreline around toward the beach and realized I needed to get to more shallow waters before I exhausted myself completely.

Along the coast, near the beach, I was neck deep in the water when I began to feel the familiarity of the earth beneath my feet. I dipped my head under and relished planting my toes deep into the muddy, grainy sediment. I brought my head above the water and stood neck deep once again, allowing the waves to push my body back and forth with their ebb and flow. Just when the waves would propel me forward, and I would feel as though I was about to fall, they would return in the opposite direction and stand me upright.

When I finally decided to get out of the water, I began walking through the waves towards the shore. I was myself again! I could feel the vitality and strength returning. It felt so good to be back in my body. As I sludged through the water, I promised myself that I would never take my health for granted again.

Emerging from the ocean, I immediately felt the burden of my weight and the pull of gravity. I noticed it first when I had been standing neck deep, and my shoulders surfaced above the water. It was slight, but I began to experience a heavy feeling as I walked through the waves. With each step forward, as the water's level descended from me, I felt more and more weight. Sankoun and Moussa must have sensed something because they came running toward me from the shoreline.

When they reached me, I was about waist deep in the water and quickly realized that their sense of urgency had more to do with the fact that I was totally naked and about to emerge onto a beach full of families. Sankoun was waiving my bright, white underwear and tunic like they were flags over his head and screaming, "No Baba... wait Baba!"

I stopped moving when I finally realized what was going on. I put the underwear on under the cover of the ocean's dark waters. I was a bit embarrassed but, fortunately for me, the boys had prevented me from creating an international incident on the beach.

Once I had secured the soaking wet underwear and tunic, I continued walking out of the water. When I was knee high, and about to walk further my knees buckled and I collapsed. Luckily, Sankoun and Moussa were right there to catch me.

The strength that accompanied me throughout my swim in

the ocean had now vanished. The feeling of my body at this point was quite familiar. I was suffering the symptoms of just having experienced an intense, over the top, workout. The familiarity of my exhaustive state was comforting.

Sankoun and Moussa sat me down in the sand on the shore. They both seemed to be engaged in some competitive smiling contest. I could tell they were proud and felt some sense of accomplishment at having gotten me this far. We all laughed about jumping from the cliff and ridiculed Sankoun for not. We sat conversing for some time before I laid back into the sand. Moussa gave me his shirt to place beneath my head. It was therapeutic reclining there, allowing the sun to dry my skin. It didn't take too long before I nestled into the sun-heated sand, once again, overtaken by sleep.

CHAPTER 7

DOORWAY OF NO RETURN

a bending tree is not broken by the wind

I lay there, nestled in a fetal position, burrowed into the warm sand, fully conscious of my desire to remain sleeping. An unintelligible drone of voices began ushering me out of my sluggishness. Lethargic, I could barely make out the differences in the sounds of children playing and breaking ocean waves.

Faint voices rose incrementally in volume. The lids of my eyes fluttered opened. The sudden flood of light hitting my eyes yanked me from a dark, soothing place of complete calm into a harsh world of competing noises and movement.

The exhaustion of earlier was gone. I was experiencing a surge in vitality as I lay there on my side, arching my spine and digging my toes into the sand.

My body felt like it belonged to me once again and not to the temperamental elements, flies, or mosquitos. I lifted myself up from the indented bed of sand. Now sitting up, I basked in the joy of feeling whole.

I was so engrossed savoring my renewed vigor that I almost forgot about my other reason for coming to the

Island of Gorée. My focus shifted. I had come, to Gorée, to visit the infamous House of Slaves. I became anxious about the time we had left on the island. I didn't have the money to make return trips.

I had not traveled thousands of miles to miss this opportunity. I knew that if I didn't get up and get moving, right away, we were going to have to rush to make the last ferry of the evening. If we didn't make that boat, then we would be stuck sleeping outdoors in the cold.

I pulled myself up further into a more upright sitting position and stretched my legs out in front of me. I was momentarily distracted looking down at the sores and scabs on my ankles, feet, and legs. The sores were scaly, puckered and dried out. My legs and feet were ashy white. They looked like the extremities of a cadaver. The saltwater must have had some effect on the lesions because they weren't itching, burning, or stinging.

I took a detour further into distractions as I looked over and saw the young men who had escorted me. They were all reclining in the sand, as I had been, sleeping soundly. Sankoun and Moussa were speaking Wolof to one another, engaged in, what appeared to be, a fierce struggle of wills. Sajo was still out enjoying the freedom of the ocean. He laughed loudly surrendering himself to the crashing waves. I knew well what he was feeling in that moment. I watched him as an old man does a child while reflecting on his past.

The voices of Moussa and Sankoun filtered back into my ears. Although I couldn't understand a single word of Wolof, I had acquired an infant's ability to infer from the tones of voices.

I was quickly becoming immersed in a self-imposed state of anxiety. We needed to get moving! Almost instantaneously I was irrationally fixated on time, or more so the loss of it. The more I thought about missing a chance to visit the Doorway of No Return, the more my nerves stood on edge.

Gorée, symbolically, had become a significant element in helping me to realize some connection with my ancestral past. Acting purely on intuition, I was prey to an illogical sense of purpose in my obsessive desire to connect with the House of Slaves.

I turned to Sankoun, intruding on his dispute with Moussa, and demanded he point me in the direction of the House of Slaves. The introspective war with "time" that had been raging inside of my head escaped through my mouth in the form of the rudest tone I may have ever used with another human being up to that point in my life.

To his credit, Sankoun kept his temper in check, remaining stoically calm and, in the most serene, paternalistic voice responded by saying, "No Baba, we must all go. We must all stay together."

There was a genuine concern in his tone for my well-being. I submitted partially out of a slight sense of shame for my brusque demeanor, and also because I had no idea where I was.

Sluggishly, the young men stretched and groaned awake. Sajo finally exited the ocean, his hands and feet looking like oversized black prunes.

We all slowly gathered ourselves to our feet as Sajo stood

at the water's edge toweling dry. I got a sense that the hostile deliberations between Sankoun and Moussa were not over. Each time their eyes met, there were furtive, annoyed glances volleying back and forth between them.

By the time we were ready to head out, the sun had peaked in the sky above us and was beginning its slow decline.

As Sankoun led our little expedition back across to the main side of the island, he and Moussa continued to argue about something in their language. I did not understand a single word and, quite frankly, I didn't care. My thoughts remained sequestered by the singular objective of getting to the House of Slaves. We were moving at a nice steady pace when, Sankoun, without warning, stopped. He then turned in my direction, and agitatedly announced, "Baba... we are all hungry!"

I had done it again. So many hours had passed since our morning tea and bread. These young men were probably starving. As is my unhealthiest habit, I had forgotten to eat as well. At the mere suggestion of food, my stomach began to rumble, and lightheadedness set in.

One of the young men escorting me actually lived on the island. I wasn't made aware of this until I inquired where we should eat. It turned out that the young man's mother ran a small shop that served food in the backyard of her house.

Within seconds, we were standing at the rear door of an old, dilapidated, French colonial structure. I watched through the screen door as the young man went inside. A woman, obscured by the dark mesh of the door, met him before he got too far in and began pelting him with strong words. Once again, I was at a loss to understand, but the high, excited tone and flailing hands of the silhouetted woman were unmistakable, universal signs of a mother in distress.

The young man and his mother ended their heated discussion and began walking toward the rear door of the house where we were standing outside. He had become sheepish in his demeanor as he introduced each of us to her. She was very terse in her mannerisms and made sure that we understood that the food was not free, we had to pay. Her business was to remain unmolested and there were no favors to be curried even if we were with her son.

There was a noticeable absence of a smile on her face until I handed her the money for the food. Once the money was in her hands, it was almost as if a switch had been flipped. Her countenance shifted from mean-spirited to one of contentment, a smile even managed to grace her lips. As she turned from us and disappeared into the house, she counted each note aloud, carefully.

Minutes later, the woman emerged from behind the creaking screen door as it flung open. She was carrying a large plastic bowl of rice, a few vegetables, and sauce. Meat was conspicuously absent from the dish. Despite the meager presentation of food, the view from this place was spectacular. From the rear of this rundown structure, we were able to enjoy a clear view of the ocean as we all squatted around the bowl and dug in. It was a fast-paced, hand-to-mouth feeding frenzy. The young men were outpacing me as I tried to keep up. They were experts at shoveling and swallowing. I only managed to get three or four handfuls compared to their twenty, or more. They were scraping the sides of the bowl with their fingers, trying to get the last remnants of sauce. I left them to their competitive eating and went to clean my hands in a small washing bowl filled with water left on the ground beside us.

While we had been eating, I had kept my eyes on the descending sun. It was getting late. All I could think about was how close we were to the House of Slaves and my desire to not miss visiting there. I had an unexplainable sense that, if I did not make it to that doorway, then I would be disappointing someone. Who? I could not say. It was a sensation that continually shadowed me.

After we had finished eating, the young men took me through the dirt road maze of small shacks, abandoned buildings, and other deteriorated colonial-era structures. We emerged from behind a set of homes, and there it was, The House of Slaves. As we approached the front entrance, I spotted a man sitting outside in one of those ubiquitous, white plastic lawn chairs. He was collecting money from tourists for tickets to enter the slave house. It was a short line, a couple of French families, a few backpackers and then us bringing up the rear. Once we made our way up to the front, Sankoun acted as our emissary and began speaking to the gatekeeper. Excitation was high for me. I looked through the open gates of the entrance; directly through, and, no less than about 40 yards away there it was… the "Doorway of No Return." Intense light from the sun flooded the corridor. It was an ominous yet beautiful setting.

My nerves set my hands to shaking. I felt a desire to rush, to move more quickly. What had once been a dream was now quickly becoming a reality. Reflecting on the thousands of miles I had traveled to reach this point made the moment surreal.

I had visualized this scene many times over the years. However, nothing could have prepared me for the reality of what I was seeing, what I was experiencing.

My adrenaline infused reflections were disrupted by Sankoun's calling out to me, requesting money for the entry tickets. A bit startled, I gathered my wits about me and asked him how much the tickets cost. The man at the gate interrupted Sankoun before he could answer me and, waving his index finger in my face, said, "You pay European ticket, they pay Senegalese ticket."

"No, not again!" I thought to myself. Africa was exhausting my soul. I stared at the gatekeeper, immobilized by anger and disappointment.

Rage was feeding on my heart. There was no way that I, a possible descendent of those held captive and tortured on these very same premises was going to pay the price that Europeans were required to pay. My arteries were searing. I was on the verge of losing my mind and doing "who-knows-what" in the next few seconds.

I could not take my eyes off of him but was unable to open my mouth to say a single word. My anger was born of a desperate desire for someone, anyone in Africa, to see me. I wasn't European! My skin was black like his! Our history was intimately intertwined! I wanted to yell into his face, "I am not white!" I was possessed by a rabid irrationality for someone, anyone, to see me as an African.

The gatekeeper stiffened his wagging index finger and pushed it within inches of my nose, "No! You! You will pay Senegalese price, "my" brother!"

His voice was brusque, violent almost. This aggressive tone was in sharp contrast to the substance of the words he had just spoken. He had just referred to me as "brother."

I don't know if the gatekeeper knew it or not, but he was rescuing me from a psychological crisis. Up until this moment, most of the West Africans I encountered outside of our little compound seemed distant, aloof. I had yet to engage in a Pan-Africanist discussion or listen to someone speak with empathy on the plight of those taken from the continent during slavery. My ears welcomed the gatekeeper's words and relegated the rough timbre of his voice to a cultural nuance.

The heavy weight of anger fell from my shoulders. Slowly my spirit began to calm. I was still unable to speak as I pulled the crumpled, moist wad of French Francs from my pocket. As I focused on separating the crinkled bills, my blood cooled. I looked up and reached out to hand the appropriate amount to the gatekeeper. His jaundiced brown eyes met mine and we smiled at one another. My smile said, "Thank you," while I interpreted his to be saying, "I see you."

After receiving my money, the gatekeeper's attentiveness vanished. He quickly turned his back on us and directed his attentions to the few who had arrived to line up behind us.

I took a moment to explain to Sankoun, his brother, and the others that there was something I needed to do before entering. I wasn't trying to be cryptic, just sincere. They all seemed indifferent toward me at this moment. They were fascinated by the French Colonial era house in front of them. I detached myself from them, walked away from our small group and headed toward the left sidewall of the house. It was my moment to be alone.

All of the research and reading did nothing to prepare me for the visceral responses I was having from being so close to The House of Slaves. I was standing on the very same ground walked upon by those souls who had endured unspeakable cruelties. How much death and blood had saturated the earth beneath my feet? I walked, scraping my right hand along the grainy surface of the house's exterior wall. The walls were high, fortified. It was easy to see how they were used to keep invaders out, or captives in.

I was not yet ready to be on the other side of these walls. I needed this time to breathe the experience of timelessness that the House of Slaves represented to me. I continued tracing the path of the house's wall with the fingertips of my right hand until I arrived at the left corner where the two exterior structural walls formed a right angle seam.

As I walked around the edge of the house, nothing could have prepared me for the disgust that was about to envelop me.

I rounded the corner and stood, paralyzed, deeply inhaling and exhaling to ward off hyperventilating.

I'd walked right into a small, filthy landfill. Everywhere I looked there was garbage! The small plot of land directly adjacent to the House of Slaves was a place overrun with trash and run-off sewage. It was depressingly horrifying.

What little food there was in my stomach was pushing its way up into my throat as I stepped through the rancid waste. I was walking on, and into, styrofoam containers,

discarded debris, piles of moldy food, and the rotting car-
casses of butchered livestock. There were several goats
climbing and sifting through the mounds of waste, feeding
on mold and fungus laden scraps. The goats remained
undisturbed, ignoring me as I carefully maneuvered
around, over and between them.

This was my only path to reach the rear of the house. I had
not come this far to be deterred. The sandals I was wearing
did nothing to protect my bare feet from becoming encased
in, what appeared to be mud but was a mix of rotting food,
trash and animal flesh.

Each step I took through the rubbish weighed heavier and
heavier on my heart and my soul. How could the people
have allowed such a heinous desecration of a historical
sacred space?

All of the years I had read and listened to people talk about
this place; I could never have imagined this level of defile-
ment and disrespect. I was standing in the middle of a
putrid landfill that might, at one time, have been a mass
grave for those unable to survive the grotesque inhumani-
ties of their enslavement. I stopped, paused for a moment,
ankle-deep in filth, contemplating the complete and utter
debasement of a people's traumatic legacy.

I quickly began to realize that the House of Slaves was neither a sacred site nor place of pilgrimage for those, like me,
seeking to regain some connection to a decimated past. It
was a tourist destination, a casualty of profit motives, sub-
ject to all of the typical norms of such a venture.

I knew something in me had shifted as I waded through
the rotting refuse. In the United States I never could have

done such a thing, but here I was not even thinking about the potential diseases, parasites or hazardous microorganisms. I ventured down a small incline, away from the landfill, toward the rear of the house.

I had made it. I stood there at the rear corner of the house for a few moments, turning my back on the noxious irreverence I had just waded through. I looked out to my left as I rested my right hand against the wall and allowed my eyes to drink in the vast expanse of ocean that served as the house's backyard.

At the rear of the house is a very thin strip of shore separating the waves of the sea from touching the bottom of the house's wall. I could see by the water markings on the rear wall that the water levels varied, reaching really high up at times.

On this day, I was fortunate enough to be able to walk along the thin, shoulder width strip of gravel and moist sand. I turned my body sideways to navigate the path along the wall, trying to avoid the lapping waves. I searched the back of the house, looking up as I sidestepped along the narrow path. I was searching for the object of my quest. I kept moving and looking up until, finally, there it was! Only a few feet away and about a foot over my head, the infamous "Doorway of No Return."

It was obvious that this doorway was never meant for walking into from the outside. It was constructed to meet the ocean with a gangplank over which enslaved souls would walk to board the boats and ships. The various water lines that denoted different levels of the sea stained the wall like the age rings of a tree trunk.

After a bit more maneuvering, I was finally standing beneath the precipice of the doorway. I had to extend my arms fully to get my wrist and hands over the lower part of the ledge that jutted out. I breathed deeply as I gripped at the narrow cement ledge extending from the doorway and slowly exhaled as I began struggling to pull myself up. In a fit of annoyance, I kicked my sandals off and used my bare feet for more traction in helping me scale the wall. To anyone witnessing my awkward clamber up the rear wall, I'm sure that I looked crazed.

The smell of the salt water, the coarse exterior wall scraping against the skin of my belly as I struggled, gave rise to a tangle of emotions. I was feeling as though I was standing outside of myself, witnessing someone else trying to climb the rear wall. I didn't have the calm, or cool, to maintain my composure. I was helplessly impassioned. Had I calmed myself a bit, I might have had an easier time of scaling the wall. A tonic of adrenaline and blood was racing through my veins as I struggled to get my chest slightly above the ledge. I was slipping, in desperate need of help as my arms and legs began that slow burn of muscles fatiguing.

I didn't need this moment to make sense to anyone but me. This passageway had been a place of misery, a site through which people walked out and into slavery, never a chance to return. This was a simple ritual, but one I felt I had no choice but to perform. I would enter through the opposite side of the doorway, armed only with a strong sense of hope. I wanted my actions to counter the desperation and hopelessness that must have been suffered by those who crossed the doorway's threshold in previous centuries.

I was not deluded into thinking that I was making some

monumental effort or statement. What I did know, and felt within myself, was that somewhere, somehow, some tortured soul might finally rest in peace, or find a measure of relief in my efforts. Following hundreds of years of grievous brutality, the ritualizing of a collective experience, reversing the order of entry across a fatal threshold was my sole task.

My objective was to return through the Doorway of No Return and complete my visit by exiting through the house's front entrance. I wanted to peacefully, symbolically, stand upright and tall moving in the opposite direction of the men, women, and children who had suffered in the House of Slaves.

The muscles in my arms were starting to cramp. A few times I slipped and had to start all over again. Each time my belly scraped the jagged stone surface of the wall; the scratches grew deeper and more painful. I continued scuttling my bare feet against the wall trying to gain traction. I wrestled against the weight of myself, barely able to pull my torso up over the side of the ledge. I was less than a few inches from the actual doorway; I could now see it. Propping myself up on my elbows with the rest of my body dangling over the side, I was able to look down through the corridor. I could see Sankoun, his brothers and the other young men standing in the courtyard near the front entrance. Sajo was the first to spot me. He began waving emphatically in my direction, alerting the others as to my whereabouts. They all came running down the dark corridor toward me.

I continued lifting myself until my waist was above the plane of the ledge. I kicked my bare knees up onto the cement, only inches away from the doorway. I pushed myself up, gasping for air. My lungs were on fire.

Finally standing on the ledge, bent at the waist trying to catch my breath, I waved Sankoun and the others off. I still needed to be left alone. I looked back over the ledge and down. The Atlantic had claimed my sandals; they were floating on the waves several yards out, and away from the rear wall.

I closed my eyes, breathing deeply, hearing the waves of the ocean as they lapped against the shore. I wanted this moment to last, to remain just as it was. It felt painfully perfect. All around me the haunting apparitions of slave ships rocked atop the waves offshore. Shadows of canoes overflowing with dark bodies headed out toward the ships.

All of a sudden it felt as though the earth was moving beneath me. Vertigo forced me to kneel down in the doorway. I remained that way for a while, emptied of thoughts. Finally, after what seemed like several minutes, my balance restored itself.

Sluggishly, cautiously, I lifted myself upright, inhaling and exhaling as deeply as my lungs would allow. Slowly, purposefully I stepped over the doorway's threshold and entered the passageway, leading with my heart.

CHAPTER 8

AN UGLY AMERICAN

if you go to the home of a frog, act as a frog

I hadn't been aware of it at the time, but Sajo had been taking pictures of my attempts to scale the small terrace of the doorway. When I finally completed my moment and allowed the boys to come over, it seemed as if Sajo couldn't wait. He couldn't contain his excitement. He came barreling towards me, running like a child unable to control his enthusiasm. "Look, Baba, look!" he kept yelling. He made it to my side and almost knocked me back through the doorway.

"Look Baba... look at these!" he shouted.

The physical exertion of pulling myself up, over, and onto the doorway's entrance had left me exhausted. I was not in a frame of mind to view the pictures he had taken, but the exuberance lighting his eyes and face left me no choice. When I attempted to take the camera away from him so that I could look at the screen of images, Sajo jerked his hands away, tightening his grip.

He had shot four different images, two of them of the empty passageway leading to the Doorway of No Return and the other two of me crouched in the doorway. All of the images looked as if they had been modified with filters to achieve a surreal effect, but they hadn't. The photos he had taken of the empty passageway possessed a very distinctive contrast between the natural light coming through the doorway and the dark, threatening stones of the floor and walls. In the photos, an animated, aggressive white light flooded the entrance. The shadows leading deeper into the passageway appeared to consume the sun's rays.

The images of me seemed phantasmal, transparent even. I stared at the pictures for a few seconds before, without warning, Sajo yanked the camera away and darted around the corridor showing his brothers and the other young men his newfound artistry.

We were all standing in the passageway that led out through the Doorway of No Return. Above our heads were the main house and living quarters. Below the main house were a few corridors similar to the one we were standing in and holding cells for the enslaved.

I walked along the moist corridor beneath the main stairways connecting it to the upper house. As I walked, I ran my fingertips along the rough stone masonry beaded with dew. There had been stones of every size, shape and color used to pave this corridor. The stones beneath my bare feet were cold and wet, but very smooth. They had been worn down by the thousands upon thousands of enslaved souls who had tread the very same earth I was now walking. I had to be careful as I moved through the dark passageway. There were a few renegade stones whose sharp edges were jutting up.

As I exited from beneath the beautiful oval stairways that ran parallel to one another leading upstairs, Sankoun stood in front of me.

"Baba, where are your shoes?" he asked in an almost demanding tone.

I loved the way that every time someone spoke to me, they began their sentences with my name. It was almost as if there was the potential for confusion if my name wasn't spoken at the beginning of any address. I pointed out towards the doorway and explained that my shoes had fallen off when I was climbing the wall.

Sankoun just stood before me shaking his head in disbelief while shrugging his shoulders in a defeated manner. I guess his father, Bouba, had ordered him to make sure to watch over and take care of me. I was making his mission nearly impossible. I could tell that he was doing everything he could to try and make sense of my actions, but he couldn't. I could relate.

When I used to get up at 4 or 5 am to practice my kora at a friend's place in Los Angeles, I remember seeing an elderly woman from Guinea who used to get up early as well. She would go outside and start sweeping the porch, sidewalks and streets in front of her duplex while singing. She had a large bucket of water that she dipped the broom in and would wave the broom above her head before placing it on the ground to sweep. Initially, her morning ritual perplexed me until I was taught, years later, she was chasing the evil spirits away who had gathered during the night and preparing a path for her family to have a good day ahead of them.

I was as much an anomaly to Sankoun as that woman had been to me.

A few yards away, there were several men approaching tourists. They were shouting, selling their expertise as guides for tours through the House of Slaves. I waved each of them off. I wanted my experience to be my own, not shared. Each potential guide appeared miffed by my refusal to allow them to escort me around the grounds of the house. Sankoun and the others acted as buffers for me, which I greatly appreciated. They followed me as I made my way like a tortoise, slowly through the corridors, touching and trying to savor the earthy smell of everything I came into contact with.

The passageways beneath the house contained tiny dirt floor cells for housing slaves. They were no larger than the size of a small backyard shed. The cells were segregated, separated for women, men, boys, girls and there was also one for the "temporarily unfit." I could only imagine how one qualified to be labeled in that manner.

With a degree of reverence for those who had been forced into these holdings, I bent at the waist as I entered each cell. My bare feet sunk into the cold, lumpy, well-trodden clay of the floor. I tried to imagine the number of people each of these cells might have held as I squatted in the center of the darkness. I was alone, yet felt claustrophobic. Each cell possessed the same, overpowering musty stench of mold and dirt. Closing my eyes, I moved about on my knees. Leaning against the walls; it was not difficult to feel the despair.

It was odd to me that I was having such a singular experience. There had been numerous people ahead of us when we arrived at the front entrance of the house, but it seemed that everywhere I walked I was alone in my surveying. Each of the cells I went into were empty. There was no one waiting behind me in a queue for their turn and no one preceding me. As I walked the dark corridors, Sankoun and the others tepidly followed me at a distance. They were watching my every move as though they thought that, at any moment, I might break down or fall apart. I could hear the voices of tourists and guides from above. Most of the people were upstairs in the main portion of the house.

Each time I would come close to encountering one of the guides with their tourists in tow, our eyes would meet, and they would turn their line in the opposite direction of my movements. I was being avoided! I could only laugh because, up to this point, my actions had to have appeared questionable. I don't think anyone had ever scaled the back wall to enter through the opposing direction of the Doorway of No Return.

I didn't possess an ounce of desire to venture upstairs, but I knew that I should.

Accompanied by my entourage, I went up to the main house. The stark contrast between the cells below and the living quarters upstairs was striking. The upper area had been prepared well. There were artifacts related to the slave trade, a few personal items someone from different periods of time might have owned, maps and other marine items. It was an impressive mini-museum but offered little in the way of knowing who the inhabitants might have been. The space was soulless.

I only spent about twenty minutes upstairs before I was ready to leave. Throughout our experience, Sankoun and the others exhibited a noticeable detachment to the surroundings. They seemed more strangers in relation to the house's history than I did. They followed me, but functioned with ambivalence, displaying a disassociation that might as well had us visiting any old house in Senegal.

As we descended the cement spiral staircases leading from the upper to the lower levels, I had a sense of spiritual closure. Ahead of us were the wooden double exterior gates that would let us out. When I got to the bottom of the staircase, I stopped to look back at the Doorway of No Return. I had done it. The ancestors had been honored in a way that filled me with a sense of contentment. I was ready to walk out of the main entrance of the House of Slaves and leave the pain and misery behind for others to have their experiences.

As we walked out of the front gate, I remained behind a bit. I wanted to be the last to exit. When I got to the threshold, I crossed with my left foot first. I entered and exited by leading with my heart. A great sense of pride and accomplishment welled up inside of me. Had I given much more thought to what I had just done, I'm sure there would have been tears. Instead of mourning, I celebrated the triumph of the souls of my ancestors.

As we were leaving through the front gates, the man who had been taking tickets stopped me and said in a thick accent, "You first Black-American I see do what you do!" He shook my hand with much force for longer than is customary and was grinning wildly. Pointing back in the direction of the Doorway of No Return, "You first one I see do this!"

It was getting late, and I knew we needed to make it back to the pier to catch the last boat, around 6 pm.

Apparently, the tales of the experiences of African-Americans visiting the site are the source of many Senegalese urban legends. Once we were away from the house and on our way to the pier, Sankoun, his brothers and the other young men began pelting me with questions. Sajo was pre-occupied with repeatedly asking me if I felt like crying. Moussa wanted to know if I saw any ghosts in the cells. Each of them had scripted our visit according to their imaginations. I was sure that, by the time Bouba and the others heard of the trip, it would be measured as an epic, much grander than the Illiad and the Oddessy.

As we made it up the road toward the pier to catch our ferry, not too far from the House of Slaves, we decided to stop and get something refreshing to drink. Cautiously budgeting, I figured I could treat everyone to a cold drink while we waited for the ferry.

The young men were excited because it had not been my manner to release my tight grip on funds. The fact that we all were about to enjoy a nice, refreshing drink had a bonding effect.

When we made it to the small commercial area, I entered the store with my entourage. Everyone picked out their soda, and I went and paid for them at the cash register. As we were exiting, I noticed a group of well-dressed people sitting beneath an overhang of one of the eateries. We sat a few tables away from them. They were chatting loudly. I had a heightened sense of awareness of them because, to my surprise… they were speaking English, but not just "any" English. It was a cadence and vernacular that echoed a sympathetic resonance deep within me. I was so excited I almost dropped my bottle of Orange Fanta. Without thinking, I jumped from my chair and raced toward them. It was a group of 6 elderly African-Americans, three couples, possibly retirees. They were laughing and rocking in their seats having a grand time.

I don't know what was going through my mind as I jumped from my chair. In the United States, I never would have thought to interrupt a group of strangers. For some reason, this moment felt different. It is a peculiar thing that most travelers experience at one time or another. When you are traveling in the land of another people, hearing a familiar tone of voice in your language has an immediate effect on your heart strings. It feels almost as if you are discovering a long lost friend or family member. It had been a long time since I had heard a cadence and tone similar to mine and it made me feel immediately homesick. As far as I was concerned, this group had made this trek to visit with me.

I raced over to the group, holding my bottle of orange Fanta and before I could get a word out of my mouth to greet them, one of the men assaulted me with the foulest, most bitter language. He hurled a string of unprovoked obscenities in my direction.

His words felt like being pelted with rocks. I was thrown off guard, situated between being dumbfounded and angry.

The assailant continued his verbal assault. The woman next to him, maybe his wife, was grabbing his arm attempting to calm him. "No… I'm sick and tired of these trifling street people begging us for scraps!"

They all seemed to be in their late fifties, maybe early sixties, but definitely from the United States. I stood before them confused, silent… trying to figure out what could have elicited such a response from "my" own people.

"Every corner we turn," he ranted, "Some dirty low-life is trying to scam us!"

I stood there trapped between hurt and anger, embarrassment and fear. I was trying to fix my mouth to form words, but was having a problem getting them out. My mind raced to make sense of my situation. I asked myself what it was that he saw when he looked at me and then it hit me. While he continued on his merciless tirade meant to dissuade me from moving any closer and begging for their scraps, I took inventory of myself. I had been in Senegal for several weeks now. I had not been as diligent as I normally would have been with my hygiene. I was a bit dirty, hadn't shaved since my arrival. Much more than that I had lost quite a bit of weight and stood before them, my hair a wild bird's nest, sores and scabs all up and down my feet and legs. The tunic I was wearing revealed that it had not been washed or cleaned in weeks.

I couldn't help myself. I started laughing loudly and brushing the dirt off of my tunic trying to make myself more presentable. My attacker fell silent, observing the street urchin standing before him laughing hysterically. It wasn't as if the situation was humorous or anything, but my laugh was born partially from embarrassment. I was also uncomfortable with the realization that a human being could think so little of another as to speak out in such a degrading and foul manner.

"Brother," I started out, "I didn't come over here to try and empty your pockets or eat your food."

The group collectively drew back in their chairs looking wide-eyed at me. On the faces of the women, I registered pity, care, and concern for my current condition. The men all looked at me as though they were asking who, or what had dragged me through hell and back. My tone, the cadence of my voice was familiar to them. They understood, with those few words, that I was not from Senegal, that I was from some place back home.

"Hey!" my assailant blurted out, "Where you from?"

"Los Angeles," I answered.

"Man! What the hell happened to you?"

His concern was less empathetic, more astoundingly curious. That quickly, I was welcomed back into the fold, degenerative appearance and all.

They invited me to sit and I did. We talked and talked. I explained about my desire to understand our history, our legacy. They were there as tourists for two weeks but had already seen enough. Everyone talked about the comforts back home that they couldn't wait to get back to. The women wanted to know if my family back home knew that I was suffering as much as I was. The men were more concerned with details of my adventure. The conversation, at times, turned ugly, with a couple of them speaking of the Senegalese in a very demeaning and derogatory manner. We sat and talked for the better part of an hour or more while I drank my Orange Fanta.

At one point during our conversation, I became very uneasy with its negative tone and direction concerning our host country and its people. We were not here for the same reasons, or the same purpose. I looked back over my shoulder and saw Sankoun, Moussa and Sajo sitting quietly with the other three young men. I had completely forgotten about them!

My mind jumped into a space of cognitive dissonance,

attempting to rationalize the ugliness I was currently entertaining. Each of them could speak enough English to
understand what my newfound friends were saying. I had
been so overjoyed at having the opportunity to speak in
words and familiar cadence that I had neglected to crit-
ically observe the content of our conversation. Not once
during their moments of speaking negatively about Senegalese people did I interrupt, or attempt to correct them.
The Cissoko family had opened up their home to me and
I had not even had the decency to defend their honor with
people who were basically more strangers to me than they
were.

As we were departing one another's company, there were
the polite, obligatory apologies. We didn't exchange information or agree to stay in touch. I needed to redeem myself
with the young men. They had shown nothing but kindness
and concern for me during my time in Senegal. Disappointment registered in each of their eyes. I had no words. There
was no way to describe the shame, the heartache I was
experiencing.

The horn to board the ferry sounded and everyone around
the pier started walking in the direction of the boat. Before
we stood up I asked Sankoun and the others if any of them
wanted another drink. It was a weak gesture of an apol-
ogy but it was all I could gather at the moment. They all
answered no and walked ahead of me toward the ferry.

We boarded and I sat to the rear with my group. The
African-American tourists got the choicest seats, the most
comfortable. Everyone seemed to know their place, even if
areas weren't designated. Returning on the ferry were people who worked on the island but didn't live there. There
were people returning from the island who had gone to

visit with relatives and of course, there were the tourists. My heart was heavy. I promised myself that before leaving Senegal and to the United States, I would redeem myself in the eyes of these young men who had treated me with nothing but kindness.

We all sat together, Sankoun, Sajo, Moussa and the others. We didn't speak. I watched in contemplative silence as the distance between us and the island slowly increased. The ferry bobbed up and down slowly moving toward the coast of the mainland. The mist from the sea was a refreshing distraction from the heat. For the entire 30 minutes, none of us said a word to one another. As the ferry docked at the mainland pier and we stood up to get off, I stopped and turned toward the island.

I had done it, I had visited the Island of Gorée and returned through the Doorway of No Return.

CHAPTER 9

THE BAPTISM

knowledge without wisdom is water in sand

The trip to Gorée fed my need for a sense of accomplishment. If I did nothing else in Senegal then I, at least, ha made it to the House of Slaves.

My renewed vigor served me well. I jumped right back into my lessons with Sankoun. Food tasted better, the people became more familiar and I was managing to get some sleep during the nights.

It felt as if the universe had opened its heart and granted me respite from all of the challenges, or so I thought.

Time folded itself into a series of nights and nights into a collection of days. After more than a month of living within the walls of the compound, I had a sense of the rituals of daily life. Mornings I awoke before dawn to enjoy the silence, cool air and stillness of the earth.

Most of the women in the surrounding compounds were up before me. It didn't seem as if these women ever slept. They moved about, silhouetted by the light of the moon. The cadence of brittle broom straws beating the ground echoed throughout the still morning air.

Their work would eventually be followed by the throaty

muezzin ushering in the rising sun. His garbled voice blared from a humongous, old wooden box speaker that was strung with rope, dangling loosely from the minaret of the modest mosque. His cajoling everyone to wake, and join him in prayer was forceful and relentless. The muezzin's deafening call, mixed with the strained crowing of roosters, braying of mules and stirring of other noisy animals, effectively roused all sleepy heads.

It was these daily rituals that oriented me to my surroundings and offered me comfort. I was soon to become acutely aware of how dependent I was on these patterns once they were interrupted.

One particular morning I awoke and went to the faucet near the common area of the compound. It had become our custom, Bouba and I, to meet here each morning so that he could turn the water main on for me. Water was a commodity in Thiar'oye and Bouba rationed it as one would any valuable resource. He controlled when it could be turned on, which was not often, and when it would be turned off, almost always. I could routinely rely on him to be standing near the spigot with his plumber's wrench in hand, but this time I was left waiting. I stood there with my toothbrush in one hand and the ubiquitous plastic water pot that everyone possessed to accompany them on trips to the toilet. Bouba did not appear. I turned the faucet handle but nothing came out. I stood there for a few minutes knowing that Bouba would soon make an appearance. He did not. I decided to head over to the shower area to see if the faucet in there would offer me water. I turned the knobs on the shower. Nothing but air. There was no water to be had anywhere in the compound.

I returned to the spigot in hopes of encountering Bouba.

Something was broken, out of sync, wrong even. I looked about at all of the young men sleeping on the ground. They were beginning to stir but had not come fully awake. Where had the women of the compound gone? I had heard them earlier but now they were nowhere to be found.

Time is a strange, illusionary element. In our minds, it seems to slow when we are in need but quicken when we are not. In my head I began to imagine the worst case scenarios if we were "never" to have water "ever" again. I stood there waiting. I then sat down on the ridge of the brick sink and waited some more. There I was sitting by the dry faucet, beginning to look the part of an indigent in search of salvation. Hyperbole inspired ruminations were fueling my increasing levels of stress. I could never have imagined being denied access to water. It was beyond my comprehension that there would be no water. Whispers of panic and fear began to commingle with the rising waves of cortisol.

Momina startled me when she hurriedly exited her bungalow. Her head was wound tightly in a vibrantly colored piece of cloth. In her right hand were the ever present prayer beads. Tucked under her left arm was the tattered prayer rug that seemed to comfort her when she held it. Because they were already up and about, the women always seemed to be the first to exercise morning prayer. She was coming toward the common area, where she routinely prayed and in so doing had to pass me as I stood waiting by the waterless faucet.

"Bouba is not here!" she said tersely as she brushed past me and into the open area of her morning prayers.

She and Bouba always engaged me in morning conversation before prayer. Today, routine was slowly being dismembered. The ritual of compound living that I had grown accustomed to was now being unceremoniously replaced by something unfamiliar and foreboding. Her demeanor this particular morning was that of a stranger who wanted to avoid all contact, someone burdened with something that no one could help with. My eyes followed her as she fidgeted anxiously attempting to spread her prayer rug out on the bare cement floor. It was disconcerting witnessing her quick, jerky movements. I had only seen her move throughout the compound with fluidity; always possessing an air of grace and nobility.

Like a child confused by circumstances beyond his control, I had questions that needed immediate answers. I knew better than to interrupt her during her prayers. Momina was pious beyond measure. She took her praying as seriously as even the most devout, learned imam would have. In many ways it was her prayer that sustained her and there was no way I was going to disrupt that small piece of our rhythm that still existed.

I stood next to the arid empty faucet. I knew that without Bouba's permission there would be no water. My mind began to jump hurdles and race with questions. Where was he? Why had he left the compound so early? When would he return? Hundreds of questions and not a single answer to be had.

The sun had not yet made its ascension high in the sky but its presence was unmistakably felt. The heat made the air in the distance appear blurry. Cool morning air has a very short life span in Africa. Dew appears and disappears so quickly that you might think it a figment of your imagination. It was early, but the heat was beginning its unimpeded assault on the land.

Unsettled by the circumstances I shuffled back to my room. Waterless, parched, I attempted to find solace in the fact that I was feeling much better, healthier. Gorée had helped to make me whole again. I celebrated that my attempts at learning to play the kora, the culture, and language were meeting with high measures of success. I was definitely growing in spite of circumstances that appeared desperate at times.

I stepped over the strewn, sleeping bodies of young men that were all over the compound as I made my way back to my room. They were beginning to wake. Each stretching and extending himself into a drowsy sitting or standing position.

They had not yet been greeted by the stark realization that the morning's ration of water was not to be had.

From the small window of my room, I watched as each and every person experienced for themselves the same disruption to routine that I had earlier. The spigot remained dry. Everyone seemed to need their own experience at twisting the faucet, as if their hand would create some miracle of flowing water. The morning progressed, no one spoke about Bouba's strange disappearance.

I watched Momina haphazardly roll up her prayer rug and dart back into her bungalow. This day, she didn't bring a smile or any bread to my room. There was no tea. This meager gesture of a morning meal, that I had once scoffed at, assumed much greater importance when it was no longer available.

I knew better than to venture out of the compound in search of water unless I went into the city. I had seen neighbors in physical fights over the precious resource and everyone guarded their access to it with an unusually violent ferocity. If I were going to have water I would have to travel into Dakar and purchase bottles, but that would still mean that no one else in the compound would have any. I decided to suffer along with the rest of the family until Bouba's return.

I sat in my doorway practicing the kora. The higher the sun rose in the sky, the more its oppressive heat encroached on my ability to focus. I was trying to practice but the more effort I made the less I seemed to be able to do. I tried by force of will to put all of the panic ridden thoughts of being waterless and hungry out of my head, but it was difficult.

I was beginning to feel as though suffering was an intimate, ever present companion courted by all in Africa. It seemed that just when my body was on its path to complete recovery, it would be subjected to more harangue and stress. The sun's heat was beginning to thicken the air and stifle the environment.

The sun in Africa is nothing like the sun in North America. I would even venture to say that there must exist two completely different suns for each continent. In the United States, I had experienced heat and it was just that... heat. In Africa, it would be an egregious miscalculation of centigrades to utter the words, "It is hot."

Tyrannically, the heat descended upon us. It was easy to imagine that holding your hands above your head might burn the tips of your fingers.

I put my kora aside after a couple of hours of half-hearted

practice. The heat was unbearable. I was sweating profusely and it was not yet 10 am. I went into my room and laid down on the block of industrial foam. Only sleep would allow me to escape the heat, thirst and pains of hunger. I drifted off, albeit uncomfortably, to sleep. I knew that when I awoke, Bouba would have returned and everything would be as it should be.

After a few hours, I was uncomfortably awakened by a torrent of sweat pouring from my skin. The mangled sheets beneath my back were now a soggy sponge that clung to me as I struggled to sit up. My throat was painfully parched. My mouth was a container of dry cotton. This immediate need for water propelled me out of bed and toward my bungalow's entrance. As I stood up, I noticed the weight of the air was heavy and there was an unfamiliar stillness to it. My breathing was labored. When I made it to the entrance and out from the shade of my room I was greeted by a thick wall of hot air so solid, so intense that it forced me back into my room.

I asked one of the young men seated beneath the shade from the tin roof overhang if Bouba had returned. His tone was defeated, "Bouba not here," he answered.

I became irrationally irritated and agitated as negative thoughts swept through my head.

My anger only aided the heat, burning me from the inside out. It allowed the heat greater access to my body. It was a powerful reminder that I needed to change what I was thinking. I didn't want to practice kora any longer. I didn't want to do anything except avoid movement. No water, no food and no escape from the sun's oppression.

The shade inside my room wasn't providing the comfort I needed. I wanted to just sit and allow this horrible nightmare of a day to pass. The cinder block walled room, became an oven. I decided to sit out beneath the tin overhang with the other young men of the compound. There would be no rehearsal of the drum or dance this day, and this left them with nothing else to do.

No one moved. No one spoke. The sun was scorching everything in sight and made incense of the dirt beneath our feet. Shade had become a precious commodity.

I was trying to abate my anger with Bouba, my irritation at the trials I experienced at every turn, but having very little success. I was becoming angry with myself for having made the decisions that placed me right where I was. Lack of water and food toys with the mind in a way that pushes the psyche to the brink. I had gone weeks eating so much less than I was accustomed to. I was voluntarily placing myself in harms way due to some ethereal notion of character and community.

As I sat in the shade of the overhang, a parasitic depression began trying to feed on me. My thoughts were trapped in a dark hole which I was doing my best to try and escape. My fantasy of self-discovery that I had carried with me across the ocean was rapidly decaying into an unconscionable hallucination.

As I sat beneath the overhang of tin, my thoughts got the better of me and I lost any sense of where I was. During these moments of mental escape I would unconsciously allow some part of my body to extend from beneath the shade of the tin overhang. Whenever this happened, the flames of the sun would begin roasting my flesh.

Here we were, me and about ten others sitting outside of our cinder block enclosures. We were leaning against the dry, coarse walls under a splinter of shade provided by the overhanging tin. None of the family members were anywhere in sight. Bouba, his sons and now Momina were all gone. I was left with the ever changing group of guests, some of them drummers, dancers or possibly extended family. Most could not speak English and since talk consumed energy anyway, it was avoided. Even though I sat surrounded by others, without the family present, I felt isolated.

Where had everyone gone? Why had they left me here with strangers? Why was there no water or food?

Intermittent breezes appeared as both blessings and curses. Weak sporadic winds brought a slight coolness to our scorched surroundings. These deceptively inviting wisps of air also transported the choking stench of stagnate pools of urine mixed with decaying piles of feces from over the adjoining wall of the community outhouse. In spite of the pain of exertion, we all, instinctively, found the energy to cover our mouths and noses with cupped hands as each nauseating draft lingered through.

Thousands of "why questions" were pummeling me. The more I questioned, the deeper I sank into despair.

An emaciated dog laid in a tiny corner of shade at the edge of the compound and appeared lifeless except for the rise and fall of his distended belly. His tongue hanging out from the side of his mouth rested in the hot dirt. He panted in desperation for air.

I sat with my back pressed against the gritty concrete wall, head buried in my hands, slowly approaching a dispirited tearful regret. I was thirsty. I was hungry. Why had I really come to Africa? There was comfort back home. There was food back home. There were people who knew me back home.

The youthful idealist that lived inside of me was suffering an agonizing, decaying death. I had come in search of Nkrumah's Pan-African principles that he wrote about in "Consciencism." I had journeyed beyond the safety and comfort of my home to engage the national pride of Guinea's Sekou Touré and sip tea while reading the poetry of Léopold Senghor in his homeland. Where were the throngs of students and theorists who had been tutored by the Senegalese scholar Cheikh Anta Diop? I was encountering none of the imagery of Africa I had crafted for myself in North America, and it was beginning to cause my soul anguish in more ways than I was capable of expressing. These were the thoughts I was now trying desperately to repress.

Dark clouds began gathering above, blotting out the sun, rescuing us from our inescapable oven. Never in my life had I seen clouds come together so quickly. It was eerie, yet intriguing. How could clouds develop and survive in such intense heat? They were zipping across the sky blending into one another, forming larger darker more ominous looking clouds. The sight was other worldly. The phenomenon occurring in the sky was a welcome distraction, pulling me out of my own head. None of my mute companions were as impressed with this spectacle of nature as I was. Apparently, this was a common occurrence to them. Nature's distraction was helping to displace my downhearted ideations.

In no way had my life, up to this point, prepared me for what followed.

Without warning, a vicious, reverberating thunder shook the stillness of the earth and air all around us.

In that moment I experienced an adrenaline rush of unsafe levels. Fight or flight gripped every sinew and muscle of my body, but there was no fighting nature and definitely nowhere to run.

The clouds erupted and within seconds water was falling from the sky. Lightning danced across and lit up the sky. Deep, loud thunder reverberated so hard that it made the ground beneath our feet tremble.

Everyone, everywhere instinctively got up and began running in all directions. The dog that I had assumed almost dead quickly came back to life, fleeing the massive downpour. I was the only person who didn't move. I was transfixed in a moment of disbelief. People who, only moments before had been quietly suffering in the shaded areas of the compound surged with energy to escape.

The moments when loud thunder and streaks of lightning raced across the sky were frightening. I was abandoned and isolated once again, but this time with nature threatening to do who knew what.

Corpulent beads of water were smashing against the ground. Tiny billows of dry dirt plumed as the ground became more and more drenched. I sat, partially protected, beneath the makeshift overhang, reflexively pressing my back into the grainy wall. The plummeting water beat out loud chaotic rhythms on the tin roofs of the bungalows.

There was nothing else my ears could discern from my surroundings, only the dead thud of enormous drops of water hitting the earth and the resonant drumming of rain falling on metal above my head.

My feet were exposed and being pelted by huge dollops of hot water. I was wearing a floor length tunic. I pulled it up to my knees and allowed my legs to unfurl, exposing more of myself to this wondrous deluge falling from the sky.

From the safety of their windows everyone stared out at me. None of them capable of communicating with me in English, they all motioned for me to run and join them inside. They pointed up after each bolt of lightning streaked across the sky. As concerned as they might have been for my wellbeing, no one dared venture out into the storm to attempt to retrieve me.

So much water was falling, and so quickly, that puddles began forming all over. The water of this rainstorm was heated. It was hot! I had never experienced the sensation of hot water falling from the sky. Without thinking of the consequences of my actions I impulsively stood up. There was no objective, no plan, just the hypnotic effect of the storm. Everyone began shouting at me from the windows of the bungalow. I could see their lips moving but their voices were being drowned out by the falling water and claps of intermittent thunder.

I had one thought, and it was not clear or organized. It was a mixture of sounds and scents. The word "water" had captured my imagination as though this was my first introduction to it.

I stepped out from beneath the overhang and stood out

in the open of the compound, allowing the waters of the cloudburst to wash me. Within seconds my entire tunic was drenched. The cotton cloth clung to me and became a saturated, second layer of wrinkled skin. Instinctually, I closed my eyes. The stale wafting of putrefied excrement, puddles of stagnated urine and dry dirt had disappeared, ousted by the cleansing smell of fresh rainwater. Whereas my nostrils had contracted in retreat from the bitter odor of my surroundings previously, they now flared in acceptance of uncontaminated air.

It felt as if each drop of water falling on my head was cleansing my mind of the harrowing thoughts that had been plaguing me only moments before. In that moment, I wanted so desperately for my head to join in my body's recovery.

Eyes still closed tightly, I tilted my head back allowing my lips to slowly part, my jaw to fall and my mouth to open wide. I extended my tongue to greet the water. Spoonfuls of warm water fell heavily onto my tongue, face, hands, arms and feet. My mouth filled with tasteless, unpolluted hot rainwater that streamed down my throat. Mud began encroaching around my feet, water rising to my ankles. My toes were experiencing a bath of mud and warm water as they submerged under a tiny lake of deeply saturated earth.

Had I been thinking, or any of us for that matter, we would have raced to put buckets, cups or anything out to catch the falling water, but we didn't. My hypnotic affair with the storm and their fear of its power ostensibly cancelled out any common sense actions.

To this day, I still do not know why, but I was uncontrollably giddy inside. There was a joy pushing the corners of my lips outward as my mouth alternated between a silly grin and a wide smile. My soul danced, as did my feet in the puddles surrounding them. I stamped down hard in the mud and recalled memories of childhood, carelessly, joyously being attracted to puddles.

As quickly as the clouds had gathered and delivered their overpowering burst, they abruptly stopped and tore apart from one another. The sun reappeared. It had not gone anywhere, just hidden behind the clouds.

I stood there out in the open, dripping wet, twisting and digging my toes into the mud. I slowly lowered my head and allowed my eyes to open. Hunger had not left me. I was still thirsty but no longer parched. Everyone was staring at me from the dry comfort of the bungalows. Their eyes were suspiciously inquisitive, housing hints of dread, or fear. I saw them. They were clearly thinking that they were in the presence of a fool. I continued with a nervous smile in their direction, but I think this effectively heightened their perception of me as somewhat deranged. Many of them guardedly smiled back at me but their smiles were forced, awkward.

Something shifted inside of me at the conclusion of that phenomenon. My depression exposed itself as having been a monster of my own making, a dysfunctional, codependent ally in helping me to negatively interpret my surroundings.

I did not know it at the time, but this moment would eventually help me to reinterpret my experience; it would aid me in gaining a better understanding of why it had been necessary for me to come to Africa. This was my baptism.

CHAPTER 10

FIRE EATERS

a patient person will eat ripe fruit

Over the days following the downpour of warm water from the sky, everything in the compound and surrounding area began to take on a different hue. The exterior walls that were once caked by dirt and pollution had been washed clean, revealing vibrant colors and extraordinary textures. Birds had been almost nonexistent during my entire stay, but now I was seeing bright colorful creatures overhead flitting from rooftops to trees and fences. Everyone's mood was much more cheerful. It was as if the waters that had fallen on and around us brought some sort of restorative energy with them. The scent of the air carried a crisp, unpolluted odor.

The compound now felt like a haven of security for me. Venturing out was always an event. Upon returning my anxiety would dissipate with each step closer to the compound. My relationship with Bouba was even growing. His interest in me and my motivations for coming to Africa heightened as my departure date grew near. Our conversations were always short, curt even. Bouba would come and sit next to me while I was practicing kora and ask questions such as, "Why do you only eat once each day?" or "Why do you only eat fruits and nuts so much?

I had spent enough time in the compound to know its rhythm now. I understood so much more than I did upon my arrival. I knew that Bouba and his family had very little money, but supported the community through their drumming and dancing performances. I knew that Bouba scraped together funds from rare occasions when he was called upon to bring his kora and perform for some important function in the capital city of Dakar. I had watched as the portions and types of meat dwindled with each daily meal until they were almost nonexistent. One of the things I had learned during my stay was that everyone sacrificed, I mean "everyone." There was no one who didn't give even though they may not have had much. I had witnessed grace in its truest form by people of every age. I had seen children holding a tiny piece of candy and trying to figure out how to split it in four or six ways so that everyone could have a share. I had watched adults go without eating so that children could eat and sleep well through the night. I had witnessed more sacrifice and caring than at any other time in my life and felt ashamed that I had not brought the same nobility of character when I first entered their home. I couldn't tell Bouba that I ate less so that he and his family could eat. I couldn't admit to Bouba that the one meal a day I ate was because I knew others were attempting to sacrifice for my sake. I wanted to belong, to be a part of the grace that enveloped the compound, and by not eating I was demonstrating to myself that I was capable of learning to be a better human being.

I don't know if Bouba ever fully bought in to my explanations but he respected my words and did not press further. Our conversations usually only lasted about 5 minutes or so. Much of the time when our talk ended, he would just sit next to me against the wall with his eyes closed, listening to me practice the kora.

I had been practicing with Sankoun's kora for this entire time and now I needed my own.

During one of the afternoons, I was practicing with Bouba sitting silently next to me and I asked him a question about a certain man in Dakar who crafted koras.

Constructing a kora is an artform and most artisans have spent their entire lives perfecting their craft. In Dakar there lived a man, Ibrahim Kouyaté, whose name I had become quite familiar with. I was familiar with his work because one of his koras had been brought back from Senegal for me years earlier. This was my first kora and it was beautiful. I swore to myself that, if I ever made it to Senegal, I would visit this man and have him make me another kora, a special kora.

When I asked Bouba if he knew a kora maker in Dakar named Ibrahim Kouyaté he seemed startled and asked, "How do you know this man?"

Bouba was answering my question with a question. Although this irritated me, I wasn't about to allow Bouba to know it. I was not going to allow anything to impede the growth of my relationship with him.

"This man made my very first kora. It was brought to me from here in Senegal all the way to Los Angeles," I answered.

I didn't offer anything further. I didn't speak another word. I allowed Bouba to dictate the conversation's direction. I had learned not to be overly aggressive in conversations with elders. The flow of information could be stopped if I appeared too eager or aggressive in my pursuit. This was a cultural nuance I had become well versed in after many times finding myself sitting in silence among a circle of other men much older than me. Sometimes I had been excited about what I had gained from my previous research and sought to impress everyone with what I already knew. A very unwelcome trait in such a nuanced society.

So I waited patiently, continuing to practice my kora, pretending as though I had not asked or answered any questions.

The silence that followed my answer wasn't uncomfortable, it was measured, thoughtful. I sensed Bouba organizing his thoughts before he spoke.

"This man is my family, we are like brothers," Bouba finally answered.

I continued playing, waiting for a moment that felt appropriate to speak. Time in Africa is different, slower. There is an appropriate time for everything, including when to enter and exit conversations.

"I would like Ibrahim to make me another kora," I informed Bouba, "And I am hoping that this does not offend you."

There was more silence between us. I knew he and his family could use the money that I had saved to buy my kora. On some levels it would have been respectful to he and his home for me to spend my money within the compound.

I had touched an appropriate nerve and could see Bouba acknowledging my deference as he nodded his head in affirmation.

"I will have Sankoun take you to Ibrahim's home tomorrow and when you go you tell Ibrahim that you are my child. Tell him exactly as I have said it to you, that you are my child and I am sending you to him."

Bouba stood up and walked away slowly. I knew deep down inside that I had probably disappointed Bouba because I'm sure he wanted my kora made in the compound by he and his sons. There was never another word spoken between he and I about having the kora made outside of the compound.

There are protocols to be followed when requesting a kora to be constructed. Most westerners are not expected to follow these protocols because it is a cultural nuance that deals directly to a difference in relationship to time. In the west, time is measured, contained and fixed. In Africa, it is elastic and open to constant change. The protocol to having a kora constructed deals with gifting time, offerings, sacrifices and getting to know on a deeper more personal level the artisan who will construct the kora.

The next morning, as promised, Sankoun was ready to escort me to Ibrahim's home. I was excited. I would finally meet the man who constructed my very first kora. I had a picture of me holding my kora in the States.

Sankoun and I took a cab partway into the outskirts of Dakar. To drive around in the center of Dakar costs too much money and drivers sometimes act as though they are lost or don't know the streets. Everywhere, everything is a hustle and tourists are often financially scammed by the predatory nature of the desperate and impoverished.

As Sankoun and I were walking up the street leading to Ibrahim's home, my heart began beating faster. The overgrown green of the tree lined streets and shade hid some of the dilapidation and ruin of the structures. Paved and unpaved roads intersected haphazardly. The sidewalks, where they existed, jutted up in pyramids as if they had been pushed together forcefully. The streets were a hodgepodge of brightly painted, colorful single story structures and neglect. The bright colorful paint could not hide the crumbling infrastructural damage. There were children everywhere, running through the streets playing all sorts of games, darting in and out of the many doorways that lined the busted sidewalks. In front of some of the rundown apartments, trash was piled up and burning in the street. At the entrance of many of the structures sat women stirring large pots. They were selling food to passersby or tending to the men hunched over in tight circles in deep discussions or involved in some form of gambling.

Sankoun led the way. As usual, I followed. Sankoun hadn't spoken a word to indicate how close or far away we were from the home of Ibrahim Kouyaté. As we drifted along the incongruent sidewalk, stepping over sleeping emaciated dogs, I looked up the way and in the distance, saw a man sitting against a wall. He was barefoot and nailing into a large gourd with a hammer. A cloud of smoke hung over his head and there was a group gathered around him. Although we weren't close enough to see clearly, I knew this was him. I knew this was Ibrahim, the man I had traveled such a great distance to see. My excitement was getting the best of me as I increased my pace, moving slightly ahead of Sankoun. Sankoun sped up a bit to keep up with me and I realized quickly that I needed to slow down. I needed to allow Sankoun to be the one to make introductions as this was appropriate. I slowed. Sankoun slowed. Without speaking we both understood the roles we were about to play in entering Ibrahim's space.

As we drew closer, the banging of Ibrahim's hammer grew louder. The white cloud hovering over his head was coming from a cigarette precariously dangling from his mouth. There were others gathered around him, all men. No one else was smoking, just him. Sitting directly across from him was a man playing a guitar. To Ibrahim's right were a couple of young men tying the turk's head knots around the necks of koras. We were approaching from Ibrahim's left and he had glanced in our direction from a distance several times.

When we made it within a few feet of him, he remained seated on the sidewalk with his back up against the wall, a half smoked cigarette jutting from his mouth.

"A salam alaikum," Sankoun performed the traditional Islamic greeting and then began speaking in Wolof. He walked around to every person assembled and shook their hands, beginning with Ibrahim. I followed suit, shaking Ibrahim's hand first, the smoke from his cigarette stinging my eyes. When we completed our greetings, Sankoun introduced me to everyone. It was the only break in his Wolof that I understood. It kind of sounded like this to my ears, "Bouba blah blah Baba. Blah blah blah America. Blah Badialy blah blah. Black-American blah blah blah."

It was fascinating standing there like some dumb mute smiling while Sankoun said whatever he desired without my being able to interject with any intelligence. Since he had led with his father's name, I knew we were safe in establishing the relationship Bouba wanted for me.

Apparently what he was saying was going over really well because everyone was smiling at me and nodding in affirmation.

Sankoun spoke a few more words in Wolof and then stepped back a few steps until he was standing directly behind me and to my left a few feet. I looked back at Sankoun and he just smiled. It was almost as if he thought I understood what he had just said. Everyone was sitting there smiling at me, no one was speaking. Were they waiting for me to say or do something? It was a spotlight moment, but one which I was totally unprepared for. I smiled and looked back at Sankoun again. He was still grinning at me but had obviously terminated his responsibilities. Ibrahim's smoke was starting to invade my throat and lungs. I didn't want to show my discomfort with his smoking so I tried to stave off the fit of coughing threatening to overtake me.

Ibrahim interrupted my awkwardness, *"Parlez-vous francais mon frère?"* he asked, the cigarette jumping up and down in his mouth as he spoke.

"Oui," I answered letting a small cough of relief escape, *"Je parle francais."*

Ibrahim invited me to sit on a small wooden crate, less than a foot high next to him. I squatted over the crate and sat down.

"I speak English as well," offered Ibrahim.

I was delighted to hear him utter words in English. Although my French fluency was elevated by being in a French speaking nation for all that time; I found the Parisian French I had learned did little to prepare me for the rolling tongue of African French.

Sankoun took a seat on an old wooden crate a few yards from where we sat, effectively distancing himself from the adult men of the gathering. I understood that what he was doing he did out of respect for the elders present. I had become accustomed to seeing this occur often, young people sat outside of the circle until invited in by an elder. There were so many protocols that it was almost impossible to hold on to many of them without being born into the culture.

"So you come from America?" inquired Ibrahim.

I welcomed the question with such enthusiasm that my words ran from my mouth without the benefit of any thought.

"Yes, I flew here from Los Angeles and was hoping to have the chance to meet the man who made my very first kora ... you made my very first kora... it is at my home in California. I play it all the time, even though I'm not so good. I practice, hoping to learn more. This is why I came to Africa to learn more..."

It was fortunate for me that, at some point, I caught the stream of consciousness flowing out of my mouth and corralled it.

"I have a picture to show you."

I reached into my bag and pulled out a picture of my kora. Ibrahim's eyes widened and a huge smile inflated his cheeks.

"This one I remember!" he said excitedly.

Ibrahim snatched the photo from my hands and passed it around the gathering of men sitting there with us. He began to explain how many years ago he had made this kora and under what circumstances. His excitement fed my desire to ask him to make my next kora but I knew there was a protocol to this request. I had to wait. I needed to get to know Ibrahim better before issuing such a request. While I knew they were used to Westerners with time constraints making unrealistic demands, I didn't want to be associated with that level of energy. I wanted to be viewed in a different light than others who had come from the West requesting his services.

Ibrahim asked me what I did in the United States. I explained that I was a writer and professional storyteller. I told him that I toured playing music on the kora he had made for me and that I taught speaking and listening skills in schools.

Usually, in the States, people look at me with disbelief when I share what I do for a living. Their sideways glances of inquiry are usually followed by, "What is your real job?"

It was refreshing to have my work accepted as the norm by the men gathered on this day. It was easy for them to associate my work with the work of griots. There was nothing foreign about my making a living through my words and music.

I spent the entire day with Ibrahim and his friends. By the evening, the uncomfortable newness of meeting had worn off and we were engaging one another much more easily through my clumsy French, infantile Mandinka and English.

Over the next week, I visited Ibrahim's home and spent hours sitting and talking. Each time I visited I made sure to not rush off or interrupt the flow of his home. On the uneven sidewalks outside of his tiny apartment that he shared with a wife, several children and a host of other adults he would sit against the wall starting in the morning and handcraft the necessary parts of his koras. Ibrahim's tools were antiquated but his hands were adept at fashioning minute details of the wooden parts of the kora. On the occasions I visited I would sit with him and his friends all day. There were always groups of men sitting, watching, talking or playing instruments. We would only break for the afternoon meal, of which I tried to consume very little as a show of humility.

Ibrahim and I were becoming close, but there was one drawback. Ibrahim smoked cigarettes as though it were his life's purpose. No sooner had he finished one then he had another being lit by the extinguishing cigarette. My reaction to cigarettes is consistent, violent even. It will take a few days but my throat closes up, rivers of mucous run from my nose and I get the weirdest sounding constricted cough ever heard.

I soldiered through my visits with Ibrahim and his cigarettes. He routinely offered me one, which I always declined. One day he was about to make the offer again when he stopped abruptly. His hand held the red and white box of cigarettes suspended mid air. Ibrahim's blood-stained, yellowed eyes peered deep into mine as he asked, "Why do you not smoke?"

I smiled back, feeling a little threatened by his tone and answered as succinctly as I could, "I do not like cigarettes."

My answer was not good enough for Ibrahim, he wanted me to elaborate, "What does this mean... you do not like it?" he asked, "You are a man, you must have more of a reason for not wanting to smoke."

Ibrahim was guiding me toward a path I wanted to avoid so as not to offend him. I measured my words delicately and explained, "I do not smoke because it wreaks havoc on the body."

I could see by his eyes that Ibrahim wasn't about to be satisfied with simple answers as he said, "You are not telling me anything."

Although pleasant the majority of the time, Ibrahim did have an aspect of his personality that would emerge whenever he was hungry, lacked a cigarette or was irritated by someone's mannerisms.

"Your body is weak, is this what you are saying?" he asked.

I had to have the honest and forthright conversation that Ibrahim was demanding, regardless of the consequences.

I began by talking about nicotine and its effects. I walked everyone present through the consequences of repeated smoking over years of time. I elaborated on the poisoning effects of second-hand smoke and the danger it poses to children such as Ibrahim's and those who hung around. I elaborated on the addictive nature of nicotine. I must have talked for a good twenty minutes with everyone listening intently. My words were not lost on a single soul present. Ibrahim continued puffing, finishing one cigarette and then lighting another.

My throat was starting to burn and my eyes were watering as I ended my foray into persuasive speaking.

There was a long, silent pause when I finished. Ibrahim puffed and then puffed some more as he continued crafting the kora handles.

He stopped, put his tools down near him and looked up at me. "You, your body is weak," he announced.

I was caught off guard because I thought I had given a really persuasive argument against smoking. His tone wasn't hostile and he wasn't on the attack. Ibrahim was simply stating his opinion. He went on, "Baba, here in Africa, men are strong."

I didn't interrupt as he continued, "In America, you have it too easy, this makes you weak. Life in Africa is a challenge everyday. When we are young we are taught by men how to be men. We learn to endure pain, real pain. You have never been taught this."

Ibrahim's assumptions weren't offending me, it felt as if I were having a conversation with my grandfather. I listened intently, trying not to judge.

Ibrahim took in a deep drag on his cigarette and blew smoke from his flared out nostrils and spoke, "Here in Africa, we are men who eat fire!"

His emphatic closing left little room for debate. The smoke circled his head and ascended. Ibrahim picked up his tools and started carving the handles of a kora once again. The men gathered around were all impressed by what they perceived as Ibrahim's wisdom. The conversation on smoking was done and nothing was changed. I had not been seduced into becoming a man who eats fire any more than Ibrahim was about to become a smokeless vegan.

The conversations drifted smoothly like Ibrahim's plumes of smoke, rising, shifting and turning toward other topics.

CHAPTER 11

LEARNING TO PRAISE

birds sing because they have songs

Over the next few days, I continued sitting by Ibrahim's side not making any requests, trying to be of service. I had learned enough Wolof to know the names of the tools and whenever he would ask one of his assistants to hand him one I would jump to it.

I wanted Ibrahim to make my kora for me but I needed to demonstrate some level of cultural understanding. My impulse on the first day meeting him had been to rush him excitedly and tell him how much I wanted him to make me another kora.

I was glad that I had waited. Waiting gave me perspective. Waiting allowed me to enjoy the people of his compound, his friends and family. By waiting I had sewn myself into Ibrahim's daily routine.

One evening, I returned to the compound and it was empty. The only person present was Bouba's mother and she stayed in her tiny, dark bungalow almost never venturing out. She had become more amenable to me, but not much. She still believed that I was the child of someone she knew and that I was pretending to be someone from America.

Whenever I crossed her path she would glare at me with suspicious, hostile eyes.

I went into my bungalow and sat on the edge of my bed. I played kora for the next few hours until sleep began to overtake me.

I eased into bed thinking of what I would say the next day when I returned to Ibrahim's home. I knew that I lacked the acumen to convey a true praising and respect of his craft, but I would make an honest attempt. I have found that attempting to engage others within their cultural norms can be endearing to them. I was hoping that any mistakes I might make would be forgiven because of my lack of understanding.

The next morning, I awoke a man on a mission. The morning was promising a beautiful day ahead. I had learned enough to negotiate my own cabs and roam freely. On my way to Ibrahim's home, I had the taxi driver stop at a small food stand on the side of the road. I purchased four white Kola nuts and wrapped them in a small cloth I had brought with me.

In West Africa, kola nuts come from the fruit of the kola tree and are an integral part of many ceremonies. They can be found in different shades but the red and white bear the most symbolic meaning. It is a sign of respect to arrive at someone's home and present them with these nuts. The white kola nuts are a bit more expensive and elicit the greatest response when given. I wasn't leaving anything to chance. I purchased the four kola nuts as a gift to Ibrahim.

The taxi deposited me right in front of Ibrahim's home. As was customary, Ibrahim sat with his back against the wall of his apartment on the adjoining sidewalk. We formed a semi-circle around him and sat along the sidewalk in old rickety lawn chairs, wooden storage boxes, crates, anything we could get our hands on.

I wanted to make my request at the right moment but it never seemed to come. There were constant interruptions from people in the neighborhood needing to talk with Ibrahim. His children were needing him to act as a mediator for constant battles erupting between them. Ibrahim's wife was on the other side of a large cement wall hidden from our sight but it seemed whenever I began to open my mouth to say something, she would yell some question that he needed to answer immediately. It would have been comedic if I hadn't been so invested in making my request. I tested it to make sure I was not imagining things. I would begin to open my mouth and her voice would rise up over the wall yelling his name. I would sit for extended periods of time not saying a word, and then when I would chance to speak, there was her voice almost as if on cue, exerting her dominance.

We ate the afternoon meal together, Ibrahim, me and three other men. I helped Ibrahim with some filing and sharpening of tools. For days I'd been willingly subjecting myself to the fumes of his chain-smoking. My immune system's defenses were now weakened. The cigarette smoke felt as though it was burning away the lining of my esophagus. I was literally in pain whenever I would swallow. Mucous flowed like a thick, polluted stream from my nostrils but I stayed. As irrational as it may sound now, I had reasoned that this was the necessary sacrifice in order to have him craft my kora.

About mid afternoon, there was a lull in the conversation.

There was complete silence all around us. I couldn't believe it. I eased into the silence with my request by asking the seven or eight assembled men, "Is there anyone who makes a kora as beautiful as Ibrahim Kouyaté?"

Everyone present responded to my question with, "No... Never..." A few supporting comments were made as extra assurance.

I was ready. I had prepared my praise in typical griot fashion and established a rhythmic, sing-song pattern as I spoke.

"Ibrahim Kouyaté's hands do not belong to him, they are blessed by God!"

The crowd chimed in enthusiastically, everyone knew what I was doing.

"All of the great musicians come to Ibrahim for their instruments because they want the best!"

More supporting comments, more extemporaneous praise for Ibrahim from the crowd.

"I have sat here for days and still do not comprehend the complexity of this man's work!"

Words of encouragement flowed in my direction to keep speaking.

"Not many men carry the legacy of their ancestors with such grace and beauty as Ibrahim Kouyaté."

I continued on like this for another five minutes or so until bringing to a close my praise of Ibrahim and his kora fabrication skills. When I finally ended, the last words I uttered were, "It would add peace to my soul if I were able to have this master craftsman build a kora for me."

The whole time, Ibrahim was grinning ear to ear. He never stopped working on the wooden handles he was constructing while I was speaking.

While I probably should have been embarrassed, I wasn't. I was doing my best to demonstrate my respect for the culture of griots and my respect for his craft.

I knelt down in front of Ibrahim, handed him the folded cloth containing four white kola nuts. He put the tools he was working with on the ground and took the cloth from my hands. As he unwrapped the cloth I asked, "Kouyaté will you create for me the kora that I need to do my work in America?"

Ibrahim rocked excitedly back and forth smiling wildly. "You… oh you.. You are a griot for sure!" he yelled.

Ibrahim handed me the cloth of kola nuts after breaking off a piece for himself. While chewing he motioned for me to distribute the rest among the men assembled. I walked around the circle allowing each person present, except the children, to break off a piece of the kola nut.

When I returned and sat down beside Ibrahim, he was beaming with pride. He began pelting me with questions, "How did you learn this custom? Who taught you this?"

Others were getting up and coming over to me shaking my hand, "You are good man," they would say or, "You have African blood."

I was more than proud of myself. I knew how clumsy my delivery had been but I didn't care. I had made an attempt and that is what everyone was respecting.

For the next few hours, Ibrahim and I sat talking about the kora he would make for me. The most amazing moment for me was when Ibrahim explained that because I was family, a griot, he could not charge me for the instrument. I wasn't about to allow that and maneuvered my way into getting him to accept the amount I had set aside in my budget.

I felt like a child on Christmas morning. My excitement and enthusiasm overwhelmed everyone I came into contact with from that day forward. My only topic of discussion was the kora I was having Ibrahim craft for me.

Each day, I returned to Ibrahim's and watched him plan the design of my kora. The day he brought back the calabash for the kora was the most exciting day for me. I held the cut gourd and examined it for cracks and fissures. Ibrahim explained the importance of starting out with the right gourd, the right words and the right mind. I was receiving more than a lesson in fabrication, I was receiving a real apprenticeship from a true craftsman.

The gourd was thick, about a quarter-inch and very strong.

"You will need this to be strong to take back to America," explained Ibrahim.

Watching the daily unfolding of my kora was like watching something beautiful take form right before my eyes.

The grainy, bumpy wood that was going to make up the main shaft and handles of my kora sat on the sidewalk for days looking like old pieces of wood that belonged in the trash.

He didn't use a single machine. Ibrahim picked up one of the smaller pieces of wood and began hacking away at it harshly. It was frightening. I could not imagine that his brutal gashing into the coarse wood was going to produce anything of beauty, but it did. Within hours the sliver of wood was fashioned into the beginnings of one of the handles for the kora, a very decorative handle.

"I go slow with making these because they each must be ready to work together," explained Ibrahim.

He spoke about the kora as if it were a living breathing person possessing a soul. Each time he began constructing or fabricating another piece he would mumble to himself. I had heard many of the older men I had encountered doing this. Bouba did something similar. I had learned that these men who did this were reciting verses from the koran. From listening and asking questions, I learned how intricately the religion of Islam was tied to the daily lives of most of the people of West Africa.

The process of making the kora took over my life. I began leaving the compound early in the morning and returning late at night. No one ever questioned me. I was so excited that, for the days my kora was being crafted, I didn't even practice. The thought of finally having my very own kora to practice with in the compound kept continual waves of excitement washing over me throughout the day.

Once Ibrahim finished putting it all together, he carried it out to a vacant lot less than a block away from his home. In this lot was where Ibrahim placed his koras to dry, to "find their voices" as he told me. My kora would need to sit here in the sun for a week before it would be ready to be strung and played.

I thought it would be better to remain in the compound than to continue returning to watch my kora dry in the sun. I considered this, but returned each day anyway to place my hands on it and, yes, watch it dry.

After a week of drying, I had my kora. Ibrahim made sure that I was the first to strike a note on it after it had been strung.

I plucked one string, only one string, and the loudness of the instrument surprised everyone present. I played another string and it produced a rich, mellow tone that danced on the air. Each time I caressed a string, it created a sympathetic resonance with the others near it. The hum of several strings vibrating simultaneously was sonorous. The kora is definitely a harp. There is no mistaking its reverberating harmonics for anything else.

Ibrahim pulled the kora away from me and stood up. He then requested that I stand. He was making a ceremony of presenting me with the instrument. He cradled it across his arms like a child.

"You will take this and teach the world the greatness of cultures here in Africa."

He then extended the kora toward me and I took it as gently as possible from his arms, cradling it as he had done.

Everyone began clapping and yelling incomprehensible words at me. I was pulled into strong embraces and patted on the back. The moment felt more like an initiation than a celebratory ceremony.

Carrying my kora through Dakar to catch a cab back to Thiaroye, I attracted much more attention. Normally I was ignored, but walking with my kora through the streets of Dakar made me an instant celebrity. People sitting in their doorways would stare and then wave. Others driving by would slow down, turning their heads. I had not experienced this the entire time I had been in Senegal. I was discovering that there was something magical about the kora.

When I got back to Bouba's compound I was expecting everyone to be as excited as I was, but they weren't. I proudly held the kora up to Bouba and asked him if he wanted to play it. He seemed miffed and waved me off. I knew better than to push the issue so I moved throughout the compound to some of the drummers and dancers trying to show them my new kora. Everyone seemed indifferent. I realized that I had probably committed a major sin by not having Bouba and his family construct my kora, after all they were the ones who had cared for, and nurtured me on this journey.

Their indifference hurt. Their lack of enthusiasm created an emotional void that left me feeling like a vulnerable child. I retreated into the safety of routine by going to practice the songs.

I sat in the doorway of my room with one foot in and the other out. I began to practice once again. The booming voice of my new kora was loud in the compound. It was truly a work of beautiful craftsmanship, so much so that everyone came and gathered around me.

It was definitely a kora that was not to be ignored. Its voice sung out a deep, angelic tone and the vibration of its strings quite literally shook the air all around us.

That evening, everyone took turns sitting with it, playing it. The early attitudes of indifference were gone. I wasn't sure why they had existed at all, but the fact that they were now gone was comforting. The thing that topped the night off for me was when Bouba came and played. Bouba's playing was as magical as the aesthetic and sound quality of the instrument. When Bouba played there was a part of him that escaped our surroundings and took flight. I loved listening to Bouba's playing and, on this harp, I could feel the string's vibrations in my bones.

I had spent years yearning for an identity that connected me to my ancestors. My playing of the kora was providing me that connection. My life and career as a writer and storyteller now held greater depth and meaning because of the sacrifices I had been willing to make. What had started as a simple desire to use the instrument for meditation and reconnection had grown into something much stronger. The kora oriented me. I had a better understanding than ever before of who I was and my path. I was not simply an entertainer, educator, or musician, I was a griot.

When it was time for me to call it a night, it was difficult to go to sleep. I had placed the kora in the corner, near my headboard. I attempted to close my eyes and sleep but the need to stare at my new kora kept waking me. I laid there on my side staring at my kora in the corner as the night drifted on.

A few times, I even got up and sat on the edge of my bed and attempted to play the instrument some more but it was just too loud. Even when I gently touched the strings, trying to play quietly, the sounds were too strong. It was probably 2 am when I finally drifted off to sleep.

In the morning, I woke in the same position I had fallen asleep in, facing the kora. It was the first thing my eyes opened to and I couldn't wait to begin the day by playing it.

CHAPTER 12

BOUBA SPEAKS

where there is bending there will be rising up

I probably should have been suspicious when Bouba began spending more time around me while I practiced kora. Up to this point, our interactions had been cordial, but for the most part, curt. Bouba began sitting next to me while I practiced and he would hum the tunes I was playing. We talked very little. Every once in a while he would correct the combinations of strings I was playing or the tempo, but usually we just sat with only the sounds of the kora and his humming breaking up the silence.

On this particular afternoon, Bouba explained that he wanted to tell me a story. He wanted to know if I wanted to hear his story. I wasn't about to tell Bouba no, but I was really engrossed in learning the traditional song I was trying to play. Without hesitation, but painfully so, I put my kora aside demonstrating to Bouba that I was excited to hear his story.

We sat side by side against the exterior wall of my room as Bouba began his tale.

"When I was a boy I told my father that I wanted to be a korafola, someone who has mastered the kora. He didn't like this and told me that his desire was for me to go to school. I was stubborn and my father knew this so he explained that to master the art of the griot, I must travel. I must be willing to travel and experience other lands, other people."

Bouba just kept looking straight ahead as he spoke.

"When I came of age, my father gave me consent to leave and live elsewhere, so that I could learn from others. He didn't just want me to learn kora he wanted me to learn of other cultures. I chose to go to Guinea. I don't know why I chose Guinea, I just did. I was young and many of my decisions did not make sense. I lived in a village with people who knew my father, our family. I did not know any of them, they were all strangers to me but my family had prepared me by teaching appropriate ways to conduct myself when I was away from home."

A flip book of images were rapidly turning pages in my head. Bouba as a young person? I couldn't even imagine it! I had never permitted myself to see this man in any other way than what was presented to me here and now. This realization made me focus my attention on him even more. I had entered a childlike world of enchantment wanting to know more about the young Bouba.

"I had a small hut that I slept in, in my host family's compound. It was a very strange place to me. On my first few days there, in the evening, the townspeople would ring a large gong. It was loud and could be heard all throughout the forest nearby. From the opening of my hut I would see people walking silently after the gong had been rung, they seemed like they were sleep walking. I didn't know why this was happening. It was a bit scary and so I would sit in my room and not follow the people when the gong was sounded."

The story was getting ominous and my interest was really piqued.

"After three days, I had not eaten. I did not know anyone. I was lying on the floor of my hut and watching the evening ritual of the gong and the walking silent. I decided to venture out. I wasn't used to such strange people and just stood outside of my hut watching them. An old man was walking with the groups of silent people. He broke away and approached me. He asked me when I had arrived to the village. I told him three days ago. He asked me if I had eaten. I said no because I have not seen the place where eating is taking place. The old man laughed at me and explained that the gong signaled that the village meal was ready. He pulled me by my arm and told me to come with him to the place where everyone eats. I was hungry and so I followed him. When we got to the place where people eat, there were groups and groups of people gathered around many bowls, all eating. I sat down next to the old man at one of the bowls."

By this time, Bouba had me fully in the grip of his tale.

"Once everyone was squatting around the bowls and no one was standing, another gong was rung. People began attacking the food voraciously, digging their hands into the bowls and scooping out fistfuls of rice. I was amazed! These people were not even chewing their food. They were pushing fistfuls down their throats, swallowing and digging into the bowl again even before their last handful cleared their throats. I could not keep up. I had not been taught to eat this way. I was taking small handfuls of food and slowly placing my fingers to my mouth, making sure not to make a mess. By the time I reached for my second hand of rice and sauce, all of the food was finished. I was staring at an empty bowl."

I'm not sure whether it was fear or my heart that wouldn't allow me to interrupt Bouba's story and tell him that I had witnessed his sons devour a meal in a similar manner. I remained silent, listening.

Bouba shifted on the ground as he was seated. He turned his body more in my direction, his knees opened and pulled up to his chest and his hands resting palms down on the pavement. His fingers began drumming against the hard surface. He then turned his head, looked squarely in my eyes and continued with his tale.

"It was many days that I could not get enough food to eat because of the way the people ate."

"The old man saw that I was not doing well and came to me in anger. He told me that if I did not change my ways that I would soon die. He demanded that I change the way I ate or suffer the consequences. No one was going to treat a grown man like a child! I changed, but it was difficult. Trying to put so much food down my throat made me choke. I often felt like throwing up, but I continued. Eventually I learned. I changed my habits of eating and began to grow healthy again."

I thought Bouba's story had ended and motioned to thank him but he wasn't finished.

"Eventually, I returned home to my parents compound. During our first meal, I dug my hand deep into the dish and shoved a fistful of food down my gullet. My father leaped away from the bowl and stood up. He scolded me for my disgusting table manners. He told me how embarrassed he was that I did not eat like a decent human being. It was an error that I was never to repeat again. I learned that when a person travels, they must adapt to their surroundings. It is a very important quality not only for griots but for all human beings. Do you understand why I am telling you this?"

I lied to Bouba, "Yes, I do understand."

I did not comprehend a sliver of his message to me. I knew it had something to do with adapting but my mind searched for the thing that prompted him to speak to me, to share this tale. I reasoned that I would appease Bouba's paternal nature and try and figure out what the heck he was talking about later.

Bouba struggled to get to his feet, bracing himself against the wall. He shook my hand, looking me in the eyes and nodded affirmatively.

"If you do not understand now, you will very soon," he said as he walked away and into his bungalow.

I searched and searched my mind for what could have prompted him to share such a tale with me. I eventually gave up and returned to my routine of practicing.

Following Bouba's sharing of his story, I noticed that people's attitudes and demeanor began to change. Everyone I encountered was still pleasant but beneath their facades of pleasantry was a sort of pity or grief. I wasn't sure what to attribute this shift to and since I couldn't figure it out I just continued on in the comfort of my routine.

Bouba began bringing more and more people by for me to meet. His demeanor was less that of a host and more of someone introducing his son for the first time. I had a sense of pride that I had broken through Bouba's tough exterior. I didn't want to do anything to upset the imbalance of our relationship so I played the role as he saw fit for me to play. I met elder drummers, dancers, and performers of all types that he had worked with over the decades. They came to the compound on bike, foot, mule and every once in a while, a vehicle. There was always a constant stream of people entering and exiting the compound.

I became very close with one of Bouba's friends, a man named Ousmane. He was of the Peuhl, or Fulani people and he played a traditional bamboo flute. I became intrigued with Ousmane early on because of his gentle manner and the way he played his flute. He spoke no English, but would come and visit with me in my room while I practiced. He was much older than me, probably by about ten to fifteen years. Ousmane would sit in my room on the floor, smile and nod his head up and down. He would then blurt out the only word he knew in English while I played, "Good... good... good!"

Although Ousmane walked around the community in an old tattered tunic, he stood tall, erect. You could tell that this man had pride in himself. One evening, not long after we had first met he came to the compound. It was a busy evening, but I remember it clearly because Bouba was standing near the storage room by himself and he seemed in deep contemplation about something. Like a phantom, Ousmane entered the compound with his bamboo flute in hand. He bypassed everyone. I don't think anyone else other than me saw him. He snaked through the crowd and went and stood next to Bouba. The only thing that forced me to pay attention were how deliberate his movements were when he entered.

Ousmane didn't say a word. He stood in front of Bouba for a few seconds, brought his flute to his lips and began to fill the air with the most beautiful sounds. Bouba stood stone faced. I wasn't sure what to expect, what he might do. Ousmane had only made it through about three bars of his song when the noise of the compound fell silent. People stopped moving about and focused their attention on Ousmane and his music. It was a magical, pied piper moment. I did not know what I was witnessing, but I knew it was something extraordinary.

Ousmane stood as still as a post. The only movements coming from his body were from his chest and torso. I had never heard a song like this before and found myself transfixed. I couldn't move. All I could do was consume the visual and sounds of his flute. The melody rode the air lightly like a feather, and his blowing into the tiny hole created a form of communal harmony. I was already seated in my doorway, practicing my kora but I had to stop. There was something powerful in his playing and I had to respect it.

The music did not possess a typical structure or sustained tempo. There were moments of soft, hypnotic repetition, and then suddenly, the orchestration would leap into a full gallop forte. It sounded as if he were speaking words into the flute while aggressively blowing. The tension and release he was creating pulled me back beneath the waves of the ocean in Gorée.

Ousmane's music had transformed the compound from a

busy beehive to a meditating monastery. Everyone present was captive to his playing. My focus had been so much on Ousmane that I had forgotten it was Bouba that he had walked up to and stood in front of. Although they were only inches apart from one another, Bouba had totally vanished from my field of vision. When Bouba finally did come back into focus, I felt a small, emotional lump forming at the base of my throat. I had a reaction as I noticed tears streaming down the sides of Bouba's face. The sadness in his eyes and the stern lip he was attempting to maintain pushed me over an empathic edge. I could not help myself, I also began to cry. I did not know why. There was nothing about what was happening that was familiar to me, but my heart ached badly in that moment. I looked around the compound as Ousmane played. Bouba's son's, Momina and even some of the young drummers and dancers were also crying.

When Ousmane brought his playing to a close, it was a final note that seemed to fade so slowly that its faint sound continued to be felt long after he pulled the flute away from his lips. Bouba grabbed Ousmane and pulled him close to him and hugged him. The crowd parted ways as both men walked out of the front gate of the compound. We all sat for a few minutes in silence before Momina got up walked quickly into her bungalow. Someone, I don't know who, broke the silence with a bit of nervous laughter. Following the laughter, someone must have said something funny in Wolof because others laughed nervously as well. Another person began speaking quietly to another and then others began moving around as they had done before. There was no discussion about what had just occurred, no one wanted to analyze what had just happened. My deeply inquisitive nature was being challenged. I wanted to talk about it. I wanted to know what had just happened. I wanted to know, but this was not the way things would occur this evening.

Over the days that followed I knew better than to inquire with Bouba. I let it go. It was an experience to be had and not talked about. I was learning another way of existing in the world.

Witnessing the intimacy of the bond that music created between Bouba and Ousmane made me think of my community back home in America. Inspiration overtook me and I was overwhelmed by the thought of returning home with one of Ousmane's flutes. I had to ask him to create one for me.

When I approached Ousmane, I did so in an extremely respectful manner. My visit was coming to a close and I did not have much time to stand on ceremony. I asked Bouba if he would mind translating for me during my transaction with Ousmane.

Ousmane came to the compound to meet with me. He was a bit more formal than he had been on previous occasions. I could see that his tunic, although still stained and tattered, had been washed. It was obvious that Bouba had already told him what I wanted. He, Bouba and I sat at a small card table. I complimented his flute playing without making any references to the previous evening. Ousmane smiled, but was still somewhat formal. Bouba translated back and forth between Ousmane and I. When we finally reached the point of my asking Ousmane if he would make the flute for me, the haggling began. I was well aware of the cultural significance of haggling, but I took a different tact. When Ousmane asked me how much I was willing to pay. I explained to him that he and I were both artists.

I told him that there is no price that can be placed on the gift that he gives the world with his flute. I went on to say that I would be honored if he made a flute for me to take home and then I let him know that "whatever" he wanted to charge me I would not barter. I respected him as an artist too much to engage in that behavior and let him know it. I told him that if I could afford it, I would pay whatever he told me I needed to pay.

Bouba and Ousmane stared at one another for a few seconds before speaking. I could see they were both in shock. They had not expected me to take this route but I could also tell that both of them were pleased. Through Bouba, Ousmane told me that he would make a special flute for me. He then went on to explain how he had to go out into the bush for the best bamboo and that he needed to raid a wild bee hive to create the lip of the flute. The details he provided of how the flute was to be made left me feeling a little overwhelmed. He assured me that he would make the flute and then when he returned, the price would work well for both he and I.

It was another week before I saw Ousmane again. He explained that my flute had been prepared but in order for me to receive it I needed to come and share a meal with he and his family in his home. I felt it was an odd request but consented. My ability to adapt and move to the rhythm of the people was growing. My time in Senegal taught me to let go of the intense need to know, of the illusion of control.

CHAPTER 13

A MEAL OF MUCOUS

a day of hunger is not starvation

The day that I was to meet at Ousmane's home and share a meal with his family, I sent one of the children out to purchase a bag of white kola nuts. I wanted to make a good impression on Ousmane and his family and I knew a traditional kola nut offering would go a long way to ingratiating me to his loved ones.

While I waited for the little boy to return with my kola nuts I sat in the doorway, as usual, and practiced kora. I was becoming quite adept at the new songs I had been learning. The intense rigor of daily practice had paid off. I could now close my eyes, relax and simply enjoy my own playing.

There was a temptation to continue playing only the songs I was strong in but as soon as I felt comfortable with one song I would have Sankoun teach me another. It was unsettling, but necessary. I reviewed all of the other songs I had learned from early in my arrival and then I would spend the rest of the hours trying to master the simple phrases of the new songs.

I was engrossed in the music of my kora, looking down at the ground, but not really looking. A pair of bare feet walked into my narrow field of vision. It was Ousmane. I stopped playing my kora and stood up to shake his hand and embrace him. He had a worried look on his face. Immediately, I assumed that he needed to cancel our meal at his home. But that wasn't it.

I called on Sajo, Bouba's youngest son, to translate for us. Ousmane stood before me wringing his hands, perspiration forming on his brow.

"He wants to know if you are coming to his home tonight," explained Sajo.

I was a bit confused. We had agreed, several times, that I would dine with he and his family on this day.

"Yes, of course," I answered, "I would not think of missing a chance."

Ousmane's face brightened. He stopped wringing his hands. The nervousness that he had been carrying with him disappeared. He nodded up and down several times and spouted out his one English word, "Good!"

He had come to make sure that I was not going to cancel on him. He let me know what an honor it was going to be that I would come to his home and eat with he and his family. I felt humbled. This was truly an important event to Ousmane and my presence was going to make a difference in someone else's life. Through Sajo, I let Ousmane know that I was the one who was honored to be invited to his home.

Ousmane turned and walked out of the main gates of the compound. As he did, the young boy came running back in, passing him with my bag of white kola nuts.

When the sun began to set, I reminded Momina that I would not be eating with the family, that I would be going to Ousmane's home. She smiled as she always did and let me know that she would save me some food.

Once again, I explained that there would be no need for that as I would be eating with Ousmane's family.

There was a knowing in her eyes that collaborated with her words, "You may be hungry when you return."

My curiosity was piqued. I may be hungry? What did that mean? She continued smiling as I walked out of the gate being led by a couple of children. We navigated the dirt roads of Thiaroye, winding around the high gates of other compounds, darting out of the way of mule drawn wagons. When we finally arrived at the location of Ousmane's home, I stood outside transfixed. With children, I used one word questions, "Ousmane?" I asked. They all pointed with raised hands in the direction of the large cement structure in front of us. Surely this was not a house. It looked more like a small cement tool shed. Again I inquired, "Ousmane?" Once again, they pointed at the large open portal where a door should have been.

The structure was a large square made of cement. The entrance was dark, almost as if it were hiding something inside. The building was a perfect square of about twelve by twelve feet with a flat roof of the same material as the exterior walls.

I approached the dark entrance. As I began walking toward, the building the children turned and ran back toward the compound. It was dinnertime and they had not eaten. The quicker they could abandon me, the sooner they could fill their little stomachs with food.

I tried to make my voice sound cordial as I approached the entrance, "Ousmane?" I sang out.

From the darkness of the enclosure, Ousmane sprang in my direction, his face awash with the widest smile. "Baba..good!"

He grabbed my hand and shook it energetically. He pulled me to him and gave me a tight, strong hug. He was genuinely happy to see me. I could sense the doubt that had invaded him earlier and the relief he was experiencing now. It was so genuine that it left me feeling a heightened level of humility.

"Baba, good... good!' he repeated as he guided me into his home. I stepped over a small ledge jutting out from the floor of the entrance, the area where maybe a door had been planned for. Once inside, there was no where to go. In the right corner, only about three steps from the entrance was a bed, a large slab of wood supported in four corners by four cinder blocks. On top of the wood was a large piece of foam with a sheet thrown over it. There were no tables, chairs or furniture of any type. The walls appeared to have been painted an aqua blue some 40 or 50 years ago and were now dingy and covered with what appeared to be mold and soot. Hanging from nails on the wall opposite the bed were several flutes, waiting to be played. His floor was a roughly poured concrete with broken patches throughout.

Ousmane called out to his wife and she came into the front entrance carrying a small metal bowl covered with a piece of fabric. She smiled at me and nodded, in a manner similar to her husbands. Hanging on to the hem of her skirt was a little boy about 4 years of age. He was naked except for a piece of fabric covering his genitals. It was tied around his waste by a string. She went to the center of the dwelling and placed the bowl on the ground and stood back.

Ousmane, still grinning ear to ear motioned for me to take my place near the bowl. He was allowing me to place myself wherever I felt most comfortable, but I didn't move because I was staring at his son.

"Baba," he spoke while motioning.

The little boy's hair was a matted mess of dirt and debris. His skin was covered with so much dirt from the roadway that it looked as if he had just been rolling around in it on purpose. Whenever the little boy would move, dirt would float from his body. On his face, snot had crusted around his upper lip and cheecks where it appeared he had wiped with the back of his hand. Running from his nose was more fresh yellow goo, slowly oozing out.

Ousmane was still motioning for me to squat down near the bowl. I finally gathered myself and was able to follow his gestures. He squatted opposite me and said something to his wife in their native Peular language. She rushed out of the entrance and returned within seconds with a large metal container of water. She went to Ousmane and bent at the waist holding the container in one hand and a small bowl in the other.

"Baba," he spoke commanding my attention.

I watched as his wife poured water over his hands and he cleansed them.

"Baba," he spoke again as his wife moved in my direction. He was gesturing as though he were cleaning his hands, a sign to me that I should do the same.

I held my hands out and she poured the warm water of the container over them as I rubbed them together. When I was finished, Ousmane handed me an old tattered piece of cloth that looked as if it had outlived its use decades ago. I was starting to get really nervous as I watched Ousmane's little boy rubbing his nose with the back of his hand, smearing the yellowish-green snot into a thin layer of mucous across his cheeks. I kept repeating the mantra in my head, "Relax, relax, don't freak out, relax, relax, relax, don't freak out…"

I was freaking out! Were they going to allow this child to dig into the same bowl and eat with us? Was this place sanitary? What diseases or vermin were lurking in the dark crevices of this room? I was trying to maintain my composure as the little boy traipsed across the room and squatted down to the right of his father, eyeing the cloth covered bowl with an intensity that screamed his intentions.

He wiped his nose across his bare arm again and no one but me noticed! Ousmane and his wife were totally checked out! They were existing in an alternate dimension or universe.

His wife came and joined us. She had left and come back inside with three small plastic cups of water and set them down beside each of us. She then pulled the cloth from the bowl revealing the most beautiful bed of rice, sauce, vegetables and fish.

They all squatted there staring at me. Ousmane was gesturing with his fingers to his mouth as though he were eating, "Baba, good."

He was wanting me to start the meal. My western born neuroses were overtaking me. All I could think of was how I was going to get out of eating this meal. There seemed no escape from this situation.

I reached my right hand into the bowl and scooped up a small handful of the steaming rice and sauce and placed it in my mouth. It was hot, but very tasty. I forced a smile and motioned for them to join me. Immediately, the little boy dug his snot covered hand deep into the rice, and pushed more food into his little mouth than it could hold. Ousmane and his wife smiled in that way that parents who think their children are the cutest on earth smile. I was disgusted. I wanted to jump up and run, but that would have been rude. I was trapped!

Ousmane and his wife began dipping into the bowl, but not with the ferocity of the four year old. This child was excited and not holding back any of his enthusiasm in attacking the bowl with his mucous coated hand.

I began searching for areas of the bowl that had yet to be contaminated by the child's nauseating secretions. I had only taken one handful and was being encouraged to take another. I had no out. I could not engage them in conversation as a distraction. As a point of desperation, I thought about singing or dancing my way out of the door. If I got up and abruptly left, Ousmane's heart would be shattered. I took a deep breath and scooped out another handful from the area of the bowl closest to me. At that point the child was shoving his hand into the bowl and stirring up the rice as though it were his own private play area. I couldn't do it.

I needed to leave. I know me. If I ate another bite from that bowl I would be throwing up the contents of my stomach all over their home.

"Flute!" I yelled, pointing to the instruments hanging on the wall. Ousmane nodded emphatically as he got up and ran over to the flutes. He grabbed one and brought it back to the area. "Baba, good," he said as he handed me the flute. From the hole at the end of the flute, a huge black cockroach fell out onto the floor and tried to scramble away. Ousmane smashed it with his open hand and then scraped the remains of the carcass from his palms with the gravel of the floor.

He and his family were existing in a state of normalcy that I could't achieve. Neither of the adults were noticing the sanitation issues. I was doing all I could to maintain my composure. I was raging inside, but trying to maintain the harmony of their home.

Ousmane ceremoniously handed me the flute. He extended it toward me with it resting on both of his hands, palms up.

I took the flute and admired its delicate design. He had cut and hollowed it to just the right size. There was black soot inside the chamber where smoke had been used to dry it out. Thankfully, no cockroach emerged from this dark hiding space. The resin from the bee hives formed the lip of the opening where it was to be played. I tried blowing into it, but this only resulted in embarrassing myself.

Ousmane smiled holding his hand out. I gave him the flute and he began the sounds of enchantment that I had heard days before in Bouba's compound.

His playing in this moment had the same effect. My mind erased the degradation of my surroundings and filtered out the noise from the streets outside. I sat flat on the ground, no longer squatting and just enjoyed Ousmane's playing. He played at length for me. Out of the corner of my eye, I could see his son still aggressively digging into the bowl, scooping out handfuls of food, sucking and slurping on his fingers.

I was relieved that everyone's focus had gone from the meal to the music. I immersed myself in Ousmane's enchantment. It was therapeutic.

Night was taking over and the shadows of the interior were giving way to complete darkness. Ousmane's wife lit a kerosene lantern that was hanging above our heads from the ceiling, while her husband continued his concert.

People began gathering in Ousmane's doorway to listen. There was now a crowd outside. This man was a master of the flute!

When the song ended, he ceremoniously handed me the flute he had been playing. The crowd began clapping and yelling. Ousmane's smile was warm, but not overly enthusiastic. I reached for money I had brought to give him, but he grabbed my hand forcing the cash back into my pocket.

"Bouba," he said.

I wasn't sure what he meant, but I resisted the fight to force him to take the money. I would see Bouba and have him explain to me what was going on with my payment to Ousmane.

I stood up to make my escape. No one was paying any attention to the meal except the child.

I grabbed Ousmane and gave him a strong hug. Although we had not been able to communicate a single word, there was a bond formed between us. I respected him and his artistry and for some reason he offered me an immense amount of respect in return.

I left his house on good terms and made my way through the dark, dirt maze of roads. I retraced my steps with the children and ended up right back at the compound. I was home. When I walked through the large corrugated metal gates, the compound was full of people as usual. I was tired so I went straight to my room. When I stepped through the entrance, my heart filled with joy.

On the small card table in the tiny vestibule of my room was a large bowl covered with a cloth. Momina had left me something to eat, and even though she was not present, I could feel her smile.

CHAPTER 14

THE CHARITABLE COOK

don't give the gift of a goat but hold on to the rope

It was Saturday morning when I decided to leave the compound early and hitch a ride into Dakar. I had become quite adept at getting around by myself. Periodically, I would take these jaunts into the city as a way of embracing my need for solitude. It seems a bit ridiculous now, but all I would do is have the cab drop me off at a gas station not too far from the ports. I would go in and buy a small bag of hard candy to distribute among the children of the compound and a nice piece of imported dark chocolate for myself. I would then go and sit near the docks, eating my chocolate and watch life slowly pass by. Sometimes I would walk the streets of Dakar, not having a clue where I was going. Other times I would, venture up and down the aisles and stalls of the Sandaga Market.

No one ever bothered me. I guess I looked less than fortunate. I was invisible. I would watch as white tourists or other foreigners were accosted to buy trinkets or fabrics in the market. I would pass by vendors and they would ignore me, as long as I kept my mouth shut. I enjoyed this anonymity.

On this particular Saturday morning, I returned to the compound to find its atmosphere extremely solemn. Everyone's shoulders were slumped, heads down. Bouba was sitting in the doorway of the storage room of the compound. There was a vacancy in his eyes that I had never witnessed. It looked as if gravity were pulling his lips and eyes down into a brooding, sad countenance.

If there was something I needed to know, then someone would tell me. As I passed people, no one made eye contact. I went directly to my room. Sankoun followed me.

"Baba," he said, "No music, no drumming today."

Sankoun explained that a neighbor, someone close to Bouba had died the evening before, and out of respect the compound would be kept quiet.

It was a difficult day. No one did anything that was normally done around the compound. The drumming, the singing, the dancing and music had all come to a complete stop. Sadness was pervasive, but I think many of the youth were more saddened by the fact that they couldn't drum or dance than the loss of one of their neighbors.

As night fell, more and more people gathered into the compound. There was never a shortage of people in Bouba's compound and most seemed to arrive around dinner time. No one was ever turned away. It was fascinating to watch the level of charity that the Cissoko family extended. No matter how little Momina had she found a way to extend it so that everyone could eat. It was a miracle of miracles that no one ever left that compound hungry.

I tried to contribute by not consuming more than my fair share of each meal. In fact, I had cut back quite a bit on my eating and was down to consuming mostly nuts, mangoes and rice.

The following day, the ban on drumming was lifted. Bouba's sons resumed their rehearsals with fervor. Sankoun, Moussa, Sajo and several other young men were drumming in the common area as though their souls were on fire. Young women were dancing, jumping and belting out their songs. It never got old, it was fascinating to witness.

Bouba had a strict policy of "no onlookers." He didn't like people hanging over the walls of his compound or pushing through the gates to peek at rehearsals. Everyone in the neighborhood knew this. It was a bit perplexing to me why so many people were violating his rule on this day.

There were people hanging over the tops of the cinder block walls. There were people crowded in the gate entrance, their heads peeking around the corner into the practice area.

Bouba sat in the same spot he had occupied the previous day, in the doorway of the storage room.

The onlookers were becoming more and more emboldened since no one had admonished them to leave. They had now pushed one of the gates open and were standing in the entrance watching the drummers and dancers do their thing. The noise aside from the drumming was getting louder and louder as people crowded the entrance and walls of the compound. Onlookers began clapping and joining in on the singing.

I had been lying on my bed trying to interpret my notes

from my studies with Sankoun when I decided to get up and go out to view the performance for myself.

As I approached the entrance of my doorway, just as I was about to step out into the corridor, a large cinder block flew past my head barely missing me and slammed into the entrance gate that was still closed. BLAM!

It had been thrown so hard that the heavy metal gate bent in the center. I turned to see where the block had been thrown from and saw Bouba standing there about to pick up another. The drumming and singing stopped immediately. The crowd scattered, running from the entrance in fear.

I looked at Bouba. He didn't even see me. It was as if he were looking right through me. His eyes had a burning intensity of anger. He was breathing heavily. He was not taking his eyes off of that front entrance gate where all the people had been gathered. He dropped the second cinder block to the ground. The anger radiating from him would have melted steel. He walked past me and into his bungalow.

His sons were dispersing everyone from the compound, even those who were part of their troupe. They were doing this quietly but with an intense sense of urgency. No one challenged any of his sons. Everyone seemed to be aware of this aspect of Bouba's personality except me.

I looked at the huge block that had been thrown across the compound as it rested on the ground near the gate. If I had decided to step out of my room a second earlier, it would have smashed into the side of my head. I could have been killed.

The thought rocked me. Was life that precarious for me here?

I went back into the vestibule of my room and sat at the little card table, a bit shaken.

As evening descended on us, everyone in the compound waited to check Bouba's emotional temperature before proceeding with anything else. Usually it would be Momina who would act as a buffer between Bouba and everyone else. However, she had followed him into the room hours before and had yet to emerge.

As it was getting late, I realized that no evening meal had been prepared. This was unheard of. There was usually something, even if it was small.

Momina stepped out of her bungalow and her children quickly gathered around her. I wasn't a part of the conference, but was hoping someone would come and inform me of what was happening. They talked in hushed tones. I walked out into the cool evening air to let my presence be felt. I wanted to know what was going on. Sankoun saw me and nodded in my direction.

When their conference was finished, Sankoun came directly over to me. "Bouba is sleeping now," he explained.

That was it? That was all he had to say? An immediate care and concern for the children burst forth from me, "What will the children eat tonight?"

I could tell by the quizzical look on his face that he hadn't expected that question from me. I had never had to ask such a question before. Everything in the compound typically proceeded with a daily and nightly order.

"Moussa went for the woman who sells fish. He will return soon with her."

Within seconds of Sankoun having informed me of this, Moussa walked back through the gates followed by a woman. She was short in stature and balancing something atop her head folded in a large piece of fabric.

"Baba, you must give money," demanded Sankoun.

I wasn't ready for him to ask this of me. My funds were running extremely low and I was budgeted for the final few weeks of my stay. If I spent this money now, then I would be broke within a matter of days.

I could tell that there was a sense of shame as Momina retreated into her room, almost sulking.

The children were dancing around the woman reaching for whatever it was she was balancing on her head.

"She will want money Baba, we must pay her with money…this is not free," explained Sankoun.

I stopped thinking and acted. If they were coming to me for this then it had to be serious. I went into my room to get money. When I came out. I followed Sankoun over to the woman. She pulled a fabric covered basket from atop her head. She then unwrapped the fabric from around a large, grass woven bushel basket and placed it on the ground. She began bargaining with Sankoun. He translated for me. The woman was selling morsels of fish that she had prepared in her home. The pieces of fish were wrapped in scraps of paper bag. The aroma of the food emanating from the basket was a mixture of sweet and salty oil. I stood there in the middle of the throng of children jumping up and down excitedly.

As we negotiated each piece of fish, I handed over money. First, we took care of the children, of which there must have been about 12 or 15. We then bought enough to feed the immediate family of the compound, including a few extended relatives who had hung around long after everyone else left. Everyone was taking their share of the portions as I paid. I instructed Sankoun to have his sister Sira take some into Momina. I knew that her pride would not allow her to stand outside with us and collect food in this manner.

I quickly ran out of money. There was more in my room but I didn't want to dig any deeper into my budget. At last everyone was fed. Everyone except me. I stood before the woman with both hands emptied of all the money I had brought out. I had Sankoun thank her for me.

I turned to walk away, heading to my room. The vendor of fish picked up her basket and began following me. I turned into my room and she stopped at the doorway. She just stood there. I tried to explain that I had no more money. I had given all I could for that night. She didn't speak. She just kept staring at me.

I was experiencing an emotional intermingling of distrust and resentment. I had never met this woman, and I believed she was about to try and hustle me. I steadied myself for another polite rebuff of her advances to secure money from me.

It was then that she set her basket down on the ground in front of my doorway, removed the cloth atop it and pulled out four pieces of fish wrapped in paper. She extended her hands across the threshold holding the food out toward me.

She was gesturing for me to take the food. I was confused. I called Sankoun. He came running and I told him to explain to her that I had no more money. Sankoun translated my words and she responded to him.

"She wants to know that you have eaten Baba," said Sankoun, "She wants you to take this food. She does not want anymore of your money. She wants you to eat Baba."

Her eyes were fixed on me and mine on hers. There was a tenderness in the moment that made me emotional. Tears began to well up in my eyes. I felt vulnerable. It was a gesture of charity that sunk deeply into my heart leaving me a bit disoriented. I didn't know what to say or do. I reached out and took the food from her hands. She spoke softly, saying something for Sankoun to translate to me.

"She says thank you Baba."

I was being thanked for taking her offering. I stood there holding the food. The woman then sat herself down next to her basket in my doorway.

"Please eat Baba or you insult her."

She was going to sit there until she witnessed me eating. Once again, I was humbled by the actions of another and shamed by my assumptions. I sat on the floor with my back against the wall. I opened the first folded piece of paper and ate the fish embarrassingly fast. She smiled. I unwrapped the second piece and then the third. The final piece I unwrapped and extended to her. She waved me off and gently guided my hand toward my mouth. I ate the final piece. Once I had finished, she reached into her basket for me. I could see what she was doing and told her no, no no. She stopped and began wrapping her basket in the cloth and placing it atop her head. She was going to leave without saying another word. I blurted out, "Wait!"

She paused once again and I ran to my bedside and returned with an ink pen. I couldn't afford to pay her for her offering, but I could at least remember her name.

I had Sankoun ask her name and she smiled broadly. She repeated her name slowly so that I could write it down on the sliver of brown paper bag that her food had been wrapped in. As she turned to walk away, I felt as though I had been in the presence of a truly benevolent soul. I knew that she worked hard to earn the money to sell her food in the evenings, traversing the back roads and alleys of Thiaroye and I was ever so grateful that our paths had crossed.

My stomach was full and I would sleep well this night thanks to a person I had never met before, and might possibly never see again.

I spoke her name to myself several times so that I would not forget it. Oumou Djiba Diallo, Oumou Djiba Diallo, Oumou Djiba Djallo...

CHAPTER 15

GUIDED BY THE MOON

many births mean many burials

I had only a few more days left in Senegal. The thought that I would not complete another week in the country had me in a bit of a quandary. I kept contemplating the fact that, in a few days, I would be back home, thousands of miles away from where I now stood. It is a strange juxtaposition of emotions to feel both joy and sadness simultaneously. This is what I was experiencing. I was happy to be returning home, but I was sad to be leaving behind the people who had embraced me unconditionally, even though they had not known me. I was ready, but not totally ready to leave.

I had one more hurdle to clear before leaving. Sankoun had come to me explaining that it was customary to give a party for someone departing. He wanted to rent a local hall for the occasion. The catch was that I would need to pay for the food and the rental of the hall. A party in my honor that I would pay for. The irony was not lost on me. Looking in Sankoun's eyes I could see his longing to make this happen. He was excited about hosting a big event in Thiaroye.

My meager budget had survived my entire stay in Senegal. What little I had left I would contribute to the festivities.

"We need money for the hall rental Baba, the man wants it today," urged Sankoun.

When it came to money, it was always today, it was always an urgency. I wasn't interested in a party but I wasn't interested in struggling against the grain of daily life either. I surrendered the money to Sankoun for the rental of the hall and food. He was overjoyed.

The young people of the compound were also excited. The dancers were happy because they were going to be able to dress up in their colorful, flowing attire and show off their skills. The drummers, although solemn faced, were radiating testosterone and energy. It was going to be a night to remember and everyone was ready to participate. Everyone except me. That youthful vigor to stay out late into the night and enjoy loudness and excitement had long abandoned me. I had been a more serene person, even before coming to Senegal. I would try to attend as the guest of honor and observe all that was being done to celebrate my time, but it would not be easy.

The party would be held two nights before I departed. There wasn't an ounce of excitement in me. I spent much more time in my room reflecting on my trip or practicing songs on my kora. I was avoiding the frenetic energy created by the impending festivities.

During the day, there was a constant running back and forth between the compound and the venue where the party was to be held. Makeshift flyers, actually scraps of paper with the image of a djembe drum sketched on it and a message scribbled out below, were placed everywhere. It was turning into a really big event.

Sankoun took his crew to the venue to rehearse. With all of the young people gone, the compound was almost deserted. Momina and Bouba were still there, but no one else.

Bouba came over to me as I sat in my doorway and asked, "You excited for this party tonight?"

"No," I answered, "I would much rather stay here in the compound." My mood was serene and I was finding comfort in quiet contemplation.

Bouba stood over me for some time. It seemed as if he had something he wanted to say, but could not bring himself to speak. I stopped playing whenever Bouba was speaking. I always made sure to give him my full attention.

"Thank you for everything Bouba, you have been a wonderful host."

He silently stood over me.

"You are a good man Baba," he said.

It was a compliment from the mouth of Bouba, something very rare. I inhaled deeply and then allowed my breath to flow from me at its own pace.

"You enjoy your party Baba," said Bouba. After that he just turned and walked back into his bungalow as I had seen him do so many times before. I resumed my playing but half-heartedly. My body was still present but my mind had already boarded the plane to head back home.

The sun was exiting the sky. Soon I would be expected to be present at the venue. The closer the time came, the more

I felt like not going. It was a chore to pull myself away from my kora and get dressed.

As I was pulling my shirt over my head I heard, someone in my doorway. It was one of Sankoun's younger drummers.

"Come Baba...come!"

I followed him. He was moving quickly. I could tell the excitement of the party had already grabbed ahold of him. He was escorting me, but did not like the leisurely pace at which I was walking.

He would periodically look back at me, stop and wait for me to catch up, and then pulling at my wrist say, "Come Baba...come!"

When we finally arrived at the venue I saw that it was a simple rectangular, single-story building, washed in pink with a few windows, about four in the front with only a single door. The structure was much longer than it was wide. We walked through the fabric-covered entrance and into an elongated space. There were pillars every few feet that ran the length of the structure on opposite sides of one another. Running the length of the pillars, down the center was the long dance floor. It was about twelve feet wide and thirty yards long. It was an odd venue. Tables were set up on each side of the pillars, allowing the dance floor area to remain an empty space. Sankoun and his group had set up a makeshift stage at one end of the long dance floor.

When I walked in, Sankoun ran over and grabbed me. He hugged me and said, "Thank you Baba." I thought it was odd that he was thanking me when I was being the one honored, or so I thought. There was a table that had been set up for me near the drummers and the makeshift stage. It was early and not many people were there. Moussa brought me an Orange Fanta and set it down on the table next to me. Everyone was busy. There was constant movement. When the moon cast its light through the windows the party began. It was almost as if the moon were the arriving guest of honor.

The young girls began singing and the drummers tapped lightly just to keep time with their song. People began rushing in through the door. There hadn't been a long line, but it seemed that the crowd all arrived at the same moment. There must have been about a hundred people all trying to fit through the small entrance at the same time. The owner of the venue was collecting money from each of them and placing it in a small cardboard box. I pushed away any negative thoughts about how much I had paid and what I was seeing. It was a time for me to reflect, but reflection was not to come easy as the drummers suddenly detonated a blast of drumming that made many, involuntarily, cup their ears.

Before I knew it, the place was filled. People were watching the dancers twist, leap and turn the length of the long dance floor. The dancers took turns breaking from their syncopated groups to perform solos in the center of the floor. Different drummers took turns leaving the troop to move around and toy with the dancers in an almost snake and snake charmer manner. The reverberations of the drums made the air pulse around us.

Another Orange Fanta was placed in front of me by, I don't know who. People were coming and shaking my hand but looking away simultaneously at the spectacle of dance and drum playing out before us.

The pace was nonstop. Sankoun's group went from one song to another effortlessly without interruption. This wasn't like any party I had ever been to. There was not going to be any slow jamming, this was an all out aerobic attack on the body. It seemed like the people who had paid to get in knew the right moments to jump into the fray without disturbing the choreography of the dancers. There were points where everyone in the venue was dancing. People didn't have to get to the dance floor, they danced in the aisles, next to the tables, and back against the walls. There was not a stationary body in the place.

Although I was enjoying the spectacle of it, something inside of me wouldn't allow me to be present. I kept staring outside. Through one of the widows I could see the moon. It was a humongous globe of white light, illuminating the night. I was fixated on it. It drew me in more than any of the excitement happening inside the venue. I was drawn to it, but didn't want to appear ungrateful for everything everyone was doing.

It was getting hot inside of the building. I walked out into the cool evening air. I was met by a moon that could've called itself the sun if there were no sun. It was so bright that it excited me. It wasn't lost on me that I was excited by the light of the moon, the coolness of the damp air and not so much by the drums.

I needed to walk a bit. I wasn't thinking, I was just moving. I began walking, alone. It was a moment of solitude. The fading of the sound of the drums began to comfort me and I found myself walking further and further away, embracing the damp night and full moon. I wasn't heading in any specific direction. I was just walking.

Although I had not planned on it, I ended up standing outside the gates of the compound. I had been walking with my head either up to the sky staring at the moon or down at the ground admiring the light's reflection off of the dirt. I stood outside of the compound gates and heard the sound of someone playing the kora.

I pushed the tall gates open and walked into the corridor of the compound. Bouba was seated in one of the white plastic lawn chairs, playing his kora. The moon's light shone brightly on his instrument as he sat there. He looked regal. Sitting beside him was Momina.

As soon as I walked through the gate, Momina stood up and offered me her seat. I tried to decline but she was adamant. For her, it was late and she needed to go to bed. There were usually no public displays of affection, but this evening Momina kissed Bouba on his forehead and went into their bungalow.

The radiant moon, cool damp air and intermittent breezes blended with the sounds of Bouba's kora, producing an otherworldly atmosphere. The drums were far away, the loud singing and dancing at the hall were too distant to be heard.

"Why are you not at your party?" he asked me.

"I wasn't enjoying it," I responded.

Bouba kept playing. I felt the need to elaborate even though he had not inquired further.

"I felt out of place there in the hall with all of the loud

singing and drumming. I just felt the need to leave and so I did."

Bouba didn't respond. We sat there for what felt like an eternity before he finally spoke again.

"The moon brought you here," he said, "You came here because of the moon."

I nodded affirmatively.

He went on, "You chose the moon and the night over the dancing and drumming."

I nodded in affirmation as I listened to the gently vibrating strings of his kora.

"Baba, the moon is powerful. Most do not know how powerful the moon is and how it can help to make things happen here on earth, both good and bad. You came back to the compound. The kora called you and the moon sent the message."

I was beginning to understand, but it felt strange for Bouba to be speaking to me as much as he was. Our conversations were usually very short. Aside from the story he had shared with me or the moments he had spent by my bedside caring for me, I couldn't recall a moment of my time in the compound where we sat for more than 20 minutes.

He seemed to be finished talking. There was no break in his playing. His fingers glided across the strings effortlessly. I was enthralled. All of the time I had been in Senegal I had never heard Bouba, or anyone for that matter, pull such sounds from the instrument. Maybe it was the stillness and quiet of the evening that added to the mystique of his playing, I'm not sure. The music of Bouba's kora was a warm quilt blanketing us both. It sounded as if an orchestra of harpists had taken residence in the compound.

When his pacing sped up, so did my heart rate. When he slowed to a crawl it was arresting. I didn't feel as though he were intentionally attempting to manipulate my internal rhythms. I felt like he was just playing for himself beneath the most brilliant moon ever to exist.

"I need to tell you some things before you leave," Bouba said, "You need to understand some things before you return to America."

I was helpless to do anything other than listen. The kora's melody was captivating me. I partially heard him speak but the greater part of me was vibrating at the same frequency as the strings of his kora.

"You are not like us, your work with the kora will be different," he began explaining, "You have come here to learn our traditions, but they are just a starting point for you. Your work in America will not be like our work in Africa."

Bouba began speaking and did not stop for a few hours. I listened as he guided me on a journey through griot culture and traditions and through metaphysical principles he had learned over the years. He was sharing freely, and at one point late into the evening he said, "I am telling you things I have not even told my own sons."

I sobered from his playing following these words and listened even more intently.

Sometimes immersion is the only opportunity to truly learn something. I knew myself well and knew that my mind was taking in everything he was saying even if I did not have total recall in the moment. I knew that his words and these images would return to me at other times in my life.

We had been sitting for a few hours when Bouba abruptly stopped playing. It was a mild shock to the system. I needed him to continue. He lifted his kora and passed it over to me. Bouba was handing me his kora! I couldn't believe it.

"Now you play," he urged in a gentle tone.

I took the kora and situated it comfortably in my lap. It was huge. It felt like it had been made for a giant. I began playing one of the songs I had first learned when I arrived, a song called Sanou. I did as Bouba had done and transitioned, nonstop, from one song to another. I was comfortable playing his kora and loved the beautiful tones it produced. I was carried away by my own playing. It was magical, meditative.

Bouba began humming each of the songs as I transitioned. Periodically he would tap lightly on the back of the kora's gourd in order to slow or increase my tempo.

He began talking once more. This time he was asking more questions, dispensing less advice. He asked me about my family and my community where I lived. Bouba inquired about the birth of my desire to play kora and what I thought had guided me to his compound in Senegal. I tried to offer depth in our conversation, but I couldn't. I was too focused on trying to play the instrument. At that time, I didn't possess the dexterity to talk and play simultaneously. Bouba didn't care, he continued pressing me to talk as I played. It was clumsy and somewhat awkward but I was managing.

"I have some things for you to take back with you to America." Bouba stood up and walked into his bungalow. He came out holding a shadowy bundle in his hands. I continued playing. I couldn't make out what it was that he was holding.

"First, you must know that I paid Ousmane for the flutes he made for you. It is one of my gifts to you."

He held one finger up near my lips, pressing me not to say a word in rebuttal. I had completely forgotten about Ousmane's declaration that I talk to Bouba about the payment for the flutes!

I was struck speechless. I wanted to plead that it wasn't necessary, but Bouba's paternal power held its sway over me. I continued playing.

"Here is a bag for you Baba," he said as he placed it down by my feet. "There are some cassette tapes of traditional kora music, very old. They are no longer available. I want you to have them. Study them."

I thanked him as best I could while trying to maintain the rhythm of my playing.

Bouba continued, "I've also put some kola in there for you. Eat them, they will help you on your trip."

Bouba then held up a small book. This is a book written about my wife's father, Soundioulou Cissoko. I know you like his kora playing and I want you to have this book." He then put the book in the bag.

"There are many other things for you. Take care of everything I have given you Baba."

It was at this point that Bouba placed his hands over mine to get me to stop playing. I stopped. He pried my fingers away from the handles of the kora. It was then that I realized how strongly I had been clutching the instrument. My fingers were aching. I had been playing for a few hours. The tips of my fingers were burning and forming blisters.

Bouba took the kora and leaned it against the wall of his bungalow. I stood up.

"I am tired and it is late," he spoke abruptly.

Bouba then returned to where I was, grabbed me tightly to him and gave me a strong hug. I hugged him back. This was the first time he and I had been this close. The beginnings of tears were forming in my eyes, I choked them back.

As he released his embrace, he spoke one last time, "You will do good for America Baba, I know this is true."

He then turned, walked back to his bungalow and retrieved his kora as he entered the doorway.

I stood there in the light of that evening's moon very emotional, fighting a flood of tears that wanted to be free. It was almost as if I was in a state of shock, but I didn't know from what. It was strange to be experiencing such a rush of emotions when there hadn't existed as much as a few words between us during my entire stay. My heart hurt as I stood lost in empty thought.

I picked up the bag that Bouba had given me. It was large and heavy. I held the small paperback book of Soundioulou's life in one hand and the big bag in the other as I walked to my room. The affirmation of identity that I had so longingly been searching for in my life was contained in the gifts from Bouba. They were a symbolic representation of my connection to Africa. In my hands was a dowry to the life I was forming for myself.

It was dark and I didn't turn on any lights. I laid down in the bed fully dressed thinking about the fact that in only a few days I would be on an airplane bound for the United States.

It was dead silent as I laid there until I heard the voices of Sankoun, his brothers and some of the other youth returning. They were tip-toeing through the compound quietly, trying not to disturb anyone. I could hear them putting away their drums, bells and other instruments. It was a quiet, respectful noise they were making.

As I was drifting off to sleep, my thoughts became less and less demanding of my attention. Just before I fell asleep, I remember looking out the open window from the front of my room and seeing the light of the brilliant moon bathe the cinder block walls. I fell asleep watching the light on the exterior walls dim as I faded. It was the most peaceful night of sleep I had experienced during my entire stay in Senegal.

CHAPTER 16

ASH AND DUST

fear is no obstacle to death

The day of my departure was saturated with sadness. Momina sat closely to me on my bed, nervously manipulating a set of prayer beads between the thumb and forefinger of her right hand. Sheepishly casting her eyes down in the direction of her feet, she spoke as if she were ashamed of something, in hushed, gentle tones.

"He is my son. He is alone. America is big."

Her whispering voice forced me to have to lean in closer in order to hear her words. This level of intimacy between she and I made me very uncomfortable, but I needed to understand what she way saying.

During my entire time in the compound, not once had Momina ever entered this far into my room. The only exception to this moment was when she had come to try and help keep me from dying. With as much care and loving as any mother would offer their own child; she had nursed me through a potentially fatal illness.

Something I had become aware of during my time in Senegal was how acutely conscious Muslim women were of all things appearing inappropriate. There was never much touching, or hugging in public between the sexes. Being alone in a room with a man other than your husband might call your virtue into question. But here, next to me, sat the compound's matriarch, Momina.

"Allah has given me a gift by bringing you to my home."

"Amina," I uttered in a very low breath, not wanting my voice to overpower hers or the message she was attempting to convey. To utter the word amina is an Islamic equivalent to Christians saying amen. Although I had not experienced any spiritual conversions while in Senegal, I had learned a deeper respect and understanding for the dominant religion of the people, Islam.

Momina kept her eyes cast downward, shifting her feet nervously as she thumbed one of the hundred beads up through her thumb and forefinger.

"You know me Baba, you have seen me Baba...I do not have to speak of my devotion to Allah."

"Amina," I witnessed.

"I know you to be a man of your word Baba, I see you."

"Amina."

"If you make me this promise Baba, I will bring your name into the Salat-ul-Fajr each morning with me. I will speak your name each day for the rest of my life."

Momina was promising to include me in her daily morning prayers, she was saying that she would bless me every morning. She had yet to tell me what it was that she wanted. I only knew that it had something to do with her son, a man who was now like a brother to me back in the United States.

"Amina."

"Baba, give this promise I will ask of you and I will speak your name during Salat-ul-Zuhr (noon prayer) everyday for the rest of my life."

"Amina."

So many questions began to unfurl in my mind, but I would not interrupt her. It felt disrespectful in that moment to speak anything that might disrupt her message for me. I listened impatiently to each word that flowed from her mouth as I focused on her lips.

"During Salat-ul -Asr I will speak your name and ask Allah to bless you."

"Amina."

"I will beg Allah to clear evil from your path whenever you travel when I place my head to the earth for Salat-ul-Maghrib (evening prayer).

"Amina."

"And when I do Salat-ul-isha (night prayer), I will ask Allah to watch over you and all those you love to keep them from harm if you will do just one thing I ask of you Baba."

Momina lifted the prayer beads toward the corrugated tin roof of my room, her right palm facing upwards. I flinched unexpectedly as she pulled the right sleeve of my tunic, moving my hand into her lap. She then brought the prayer beads down and placed them into the palm of my right hand. Momina closed my fingers around the beads and then lifted her head, looking determinedly into my eyes. Tears were streaming down both sides of her face. I had not been aware that the entire time she had been speaking, she had also been crying. I was suddenly awash with sadness and felt as if my heart had swollen to twice its size. I held on to the beads tightly as she removed her hands from around mine.

"Treat my son in America as though is he a part of your family. Please protect and watch over him as you would your own blood. Baba, I beg you do this, you promise me you will do this and I give you my word that, for the rest of my days I will seek blessings for you during every prayer each day and night."

Looking into the eyes and despondent face of a mother grieving for the life of a son living far from home, I spoke.

"Badialy is like a brother to me. He has done extraordinary things for me since we met. Your son had demonstrated the kindness, care and concern for others that you taught him."

"Amina," she whispered.

"You must know that your son exudes a love for others in the way he chooses to live his life."

Amina."

"Momina, there are many stories that I should have shared with you about your son during my time here, and for some reason I did not. I hope that you will forgive me."

"Amina."

"Momina, when I first met Badialy he was not doing well because he was new to our country. He shared a small room with several other men from Senegal. They all had very little. One afternoon, when we had just finished drumming for a dance class, each of us drummers received some change in the form of donations from the dancers. After receiving his stipend, Badialy left us, running across the street to a small convenience store. Because he and I had spoken honestly, I knew that this was the "only" money that he possessed in that moment. Badialy came out of the convenience store, running back across the street. In his hands was a small loaf of cake. I knew he had not eaten at all that day and was not surprised that the first thing he would do was to go get something to feed himself. But it was more than that. Your son gathered all of the drummers around him in a circle and began breaking the loaf into pieces with his hands, offering us a portion to consume."

Emotions welled up inside of me as I shared this story, "Even though your son was hungry Momina, his first thought was still to take care of others."

"Amina," she whispered, tears staining her cheeks.

Momina began wiping her eyes almost as if it would help her to hear me better, "Amina."

I wanted to express my sincerity and appreciation for what she and her family had done for me and so I continued sharing another anecdote related to her son.

"Another time Momina, he and I were walking through the streets of the city when we came upon a man who was a dear friend to the both of us. This man had been home-less for some weeks and neither Badialy nor I had been aware of this. We stood with the man listening to his heart-wrenching tale for some time when your son looked down at the man's feet and saw that they were bare. Your son removed his sandals, bent down and placed them on our friend's feet."

"Amina."

"As a mother, Momina, you have given your children gifts that they share with the rest of the world. You have done so much for so many and I want you to be aware of it."

"Amina."

"I will do all that is within my power to watch over and care for your son while he is far from you in America, he is a brother to me."

Despondency and sadness gave way to relief as the lips on Momina's face curled upward into a smile. She had achieved what she had come for and now there was a spir-itual contract between she and I. We were now intimately connected in a way that we had not been during my entire stay in the compound. Our words formed a covenant, faith-fully intertwined with promises made to one another.

Momina excitedly wrapped both arms around me as we sat next to one another on that bed. Her embrace filled me with a warm, gentle glow that exuded her loving spirit.

"Thank you Baba... thank you."

She stood up and spoke words in Arabic that I could not

understand. Usually when someone spoke words in Arabic, they were issuing a prayer of some sort or offering words from the koran that fit with the moment. I stood and hugged Momina once more before she turned and silently walked out of my room.

This was my final day in Senegal. In the evening I would be boarding a flight to return to the United States. My room became a gathering place. I spent the entire day hosting a parade of visitors. Small crowds formed in my room, slowly dispersing only to be replaced by another small group of people. Some of the people who came I knew well, others brought friends with them who were strangers to me. Everyone had some story to share about our time together. I was praised and poked fun at. At times it felt like a comedic roast, and at other moments it felt like I was listening to eulogies at my own funeral. The meals this day were on the side of abundance. Momina had brought in a plate of scrambled eggs, bread and tea. For lunch there was a huge bed of rice, sauce, vegetables and fish. The difference this time was that I squatted with everyone else and ate with my hand from the common bowl, no big spoon necessary. Sankoun's drummers drummed for me. The dancers danced for me. Everyone did everything they could to make me know that I had been an honored guest.

Ousmane came by my room where Sankoun, Moussa, Sajo and many of the other young drummers were gathered. Sankoun translated for him. He spoke of the honor I had brought to his home by coming to share a meal. He told the gathering that he and I had been brothers in another life and he knew this to be true. I was emotional listening to him speak. When Ousmane finished, he handed me a long piece of folded cloth. I unwrapped the cloth and saw that

Ousmane had made me another flute. It was beautiful! He grinned ear to ear with pride as I fawned over his extraordinary artistry. Sankoun translated each of my words with the sincerity that I spoke them. Ousmane retrieved the flute from my hands and began playing it with intense fervor. The song he let loose was joyous and celebratory. When he finished playing, he handed the flute back to me. I placed it in the cloth and tucked it away in the bag that Bouba had given me the previous evening.

Although the face of the crowd changed periodically, Ousmane remained, smiling and nodding in that familiar manner.

I had two suitcases. Throughout the day I gave away articles of clothing, shoes and most of what I had brought with me. By the time the evening sky appeared I had relinquished all of the possessions I had brought from home. As my time drew near to depart for the airport, the only things I had left were two empty pieces of luggage, the bag Bouba had given me and my kora. I gave the luggage to two young drummers who took them with such enthusiasm that it seemed as if they had just won a lottery.

It was time to leave for the airport. I did not want to leave. A part of me seriously contemplated staying, while another part of me jumped joyously inside at the thought of returning home. Outside of my room, were dozens and dozens of people waiting to see me off. I stepped out holding my kora and the bag from Bouba. I was wearing the same tunic I had worn in the Doorway of No Return. Immediately, someone grabbed my bag and then someone else grabbed the kora from me and took them to the awaiting cab sitting right outside of the open gates of the compound. I waded through the mass of bodies, hugging, being kissed on the cheek, shaking hands… slowly moving closer and closer to the cab with Sankoun and his brothers as guides.

I kept rotating my head left to right, forward and back searching for Bouba. He was nowhere to be found. I was sad that I would be departing without seeing him one last time, but I understood. Maybe his heart ached as much as mine. The closer I got to the opening of the gate, the more I resolved that I would probably never see Bouba again.

We finally made it through the throng and outside of the entrance. When we stepped out of the gates, Sajo ran forward to open the passenger side door of the cab. Standing there next to the cab was Momina. Directly behind her was Bouba. Momina rushed forward with her arms wide and grabbed me and hugged me. She was crying once again. It was contagious. I began to cry. She released her tight hug on me and then Bouba stepped forward. He hugged me tightly, but only for a few seconds, nothing like Momina.

"You go safe into the world Baba," he said as he quickly walked around me, disappearing into the crowd of bodies in the compound. Momina dutifully followed him as I had seen her do so many times before.

The brothers pushed me toward the cab, "We're late Baba, we must go!"

I can honestly say, that for once in my life, I didn't mind missing a plane. The thought of having to return to the compound because I had missed my flight gave me some joy.

We were all crowded into the tiny cab as we had been when I first came. The old, dilapidated Peugout bounced and lurched its way through the dark streets of Thiaroye. There was a little more room for comfort this time as there was no luggage. I realized that I hadn't haggled for the price of the taxi. I had no idea what we were paying. I only had a few coins left of my budget. I was quite literally running on financial fumes.

Once again, when we arrived at the airport, Sankoun, Moussa and Sajo acted as bodyguards as I exited the cab. When the cab first approached curbside, there was an immediate rush of young men hawking their services to help with luggage or give directions, etc. There were far too many for Sankoun, Moussa and Sajo to shoo away by themselves. When I got out of the taxi to assist a strange thing happened. The cluster of hawkers stood for a few moments staring at me, and then almost as if on cue, dispersed to find someone else to offer their services to. It was strange, but I didn't have time to think about it. I was being rushed to the ticket counter by my entourage.

We reached a security checkpoint in the airport where the brothers could no longer accompany me. Sankoun handed me my kora. I was carrying the bag that Bouba had given me. It was a difficult parting of ways. None of us was comfortable with saying "goodbye." By the time we embraced and were able to part one another's company I was in deep danger of missing my flight.

I backed into the secured area waving at Sankoun, Moussa and Sajo. Turning away filled me with a sense of loss, an abrupt and painful disconnecting.

There was a heavy presence of police, security and military throughout the airport. When I turned the corner of the secured area, there was an overabundance of people giving orders, barking directions. I must have shown my passport to about ten different people, some of whom I'm sure had no authority or need. I ended up in a crowded line of people being herded down hallways and through several doors. At each door we deposited some of our lot and by the time I made it to my gate, there were only a few dozen with me.

I took a seat across from the large windows looking out onto the tarmac. I felt alone. The mix of emotions I was feeling were uncomfortable. I was in the waiting area for my plane experiencing a cascading onset of sorrow. The solace of being in my own head without interruptions was familiar, but for some reason a bit disconcerting.

"How much money do you have?"

Standing over me was a man dressed in an old, dirty pair of jeans and faded blue polo shirt. I didn't say anything, I just looked up at him.

"You must tell me how much money you have!" he ordered.

I was beginning to anger when I realized I had met hundreds of men like him during my time in Senegal. I waved him away with a dismissive tick and sucking of my teeth. He left me in a huff, angered but understanding I knew his game.

I heard him walk down toward a group of tourists seated not far from me. "How much money do you have?" he barked at them. Amazingly, they all began to each tell the man how much money they had. He was attempting to hustle them in an exchange rate scam. He was going to give them counterfeit bills in exchange for the actual currency, or just as bad, much less than the rate they deserved.

I couldn't stand it so I got up and started walking quickly over to where he was hustling the tourists. I wanted to save them from a horrible fate and loss.

The hustler saw me coming and darted away from the group. I didn't have to walk all the way down the hall to them. He was leaving. So I returned to my seat.

Sitting in the waiting area of my flight, I was enjoying comforts I had not experienced the whole time I had been in Senegal. There was an air-conditioner pumping out cool air. I went to a vendor and purchased a cold bottle of water, which I drank ever so slowly and rubbed on my neck and forehead. It might as well have been a spa as far as I was concerned. I couldn't help but to laugh as I watched two older women, American tourists, jump from their seats and run down the corridor at the sight of a single mosquito buzzing high over their heads.

As I was sitting there, I had the sudden realization that I had not entered a real bathroom in months. For some reason, the idea of a "real" porcelain toilet and running water animated me. I hadn't seen a real sink or toilet in all the time I had been in Senegal. A surge of exhilaration propelled me up from my seat. I grabbed my kora and bag and made my way to the public restroom. It was an odd thing to be excited about, but you never know what you will miss when separated from what is familiar.

When I walked into the restroom and turned the corner to where the sink and mirrors were, I lost the grip on my bag and it fell to the floor. I held tightly onto the neck of my kora. I stood transfixed. I couldn't move any further. I was face to face with my own image in a mirror. I realized then and there that I had not looked into a mirror in months. My face showing through the smeared glass made me cringe. Standing before me, staring back at me was a cadaver, an emaciated figure with hollowed cheeks, ashy dark skin and deep sunken eyes. My larynx protruded from a neck that possessed more bone than muscle. The usual caramel color of my skin was replaced by that of a seared, burnt hue. I did not recognize the ghost peering hauntingly back at me.

I approached the mirror with disbelief and trepidation. Slightly, I bent over the sink and brought my nose within inches of the clouded glass. I brought both of my hands up to my face and caressed its contours as if blind. I was in the throes of an aggressive state of denial at what I was seeing. I didn't want to believe that the shell of a figure confronting me in the mirror was me. I stepped back away from the sink and place my hands up in front of my eyes. As odd as it may sound, I had not recognized how emaciated my hands had become until that moment. They appeared, quite literally, skin and bones. For the first time I was seeing what everyone else was seeing when they looked at me.

My memories spun in reverse displaying recent experiences. I now understood why the Fulani woman had offered me free food after I had fed everyone else and didn't have enough money for myself. I now understood why Bouba had felt the need to share his story with me. I now knew what the curbside hawkers saw when I exited the vehicle and why they dispersed leaving me alone.

The imagery sputtered rapidly through my mind before completing and fading to black. I stood there a captive of the emaciated soul standing in the mirror, staring eerily at me.

I had come to Africa in search of an obscured past veiled by time. My insatiable drive and obsessive desire to connect with some aspect of my ancestral lineage now seemed stripped of reason. As I stood before the mirror looking at the weak scaffold of a man, I didn't feel weakness. In fact, as I stood there, I was experiencing a welling of pride and some sort of emergence of inner-strength. In spite of my appearance, I felt a power beyond physical measure. Throughout this entire experience I had been guided, watched over and protected.

I was returning to America not as a descendent of the enslaved but as a soul, fully awakened.

THE END

Free Music

Thank you for reading **Road of Ash and Dust**. Don't forget your **FREE DOWNLOAD** of music referenced in the book. Visit the site below to begin your free download now:

http://RoadofAshandDust.com

Discussion Guide

ROAD OF ASH AND DUST

AUTHOR

What was the author trying to accomplish?
(Entertain the reader, deliver a message or both?)

Do you feel this book included elements of other genres?
(travel, autobiography, etc.?)

Were you able to relate to the author?

THE BOOK IN GENERAL

Is the book believable?

What is the book's greatest strength or most serious flaw?

Did this book shock or disturb you?

If you had to describe this book in just one word, what
would it be?

Can any comparison be made between this book and any
other you've read?

Would you recommend this book to someone else?

CHARACTERS

Did you identify with the main character?

Did you feel he was sympathetic?

Did you love him or hate him?

What problems/challenges that he faced stood out to you?

Did you feel that conflicts were neatly resolved or left undecided?

What were some of the choices that the main character faced?

How do his decisions affect his life and the lives of other characters?

Can you think of a choice he made that stands out to you? Why?

STYLE

How is the story told?

Was the book driven by plot, an idea, or the characters?

Did you discover any symbolism in the book?

Did the author's writing style/use of language add to the book or make it more difficult to read?

Read a paragraph from the book to illustrate the author's style or special use of language.

THEME

What is the book about?

What ideas drive the story?

Is the theme relevant today?

TITLE

Why do you think the author chose the title?

Was it a good choice?

How does it relate to the story?

About the Author

E.L. Cyrs is a world traveled, award-winning professional presenter and speaker. He has garnered commendations from both the U.S. Senate and Congress for his work as an artist, cultural educator, and volunteer helping troubled teens. When not writing, presenting or globe trotting he can be found trying to become the world's greatest husband, father, and grandpa. Visit the author's website at ELCyrs.com

Thank you

Like most writers, it warms my heart to know that someone read and enjoyed my work. It is an affirmation of purpose. Thank you for reading **Road of Ash and Dust**. I hope that you will recommend the book to friends, family members, and colleagues. It would be an inspirational testimony of support if you were to write a review.

To stay up to date on what's happening with me and my creative pursuits visit the following sites:

Visit my website:
www.ELCyrs.com

Follow me on twitter:
www.twitter.com/ELCyrs

Like my Author's Facebook page:
www.facebook.com/AuthorCyrs

Printed in Great Britain
by Amazon

27524908R00126